TUNE UP YOUR TOOLS

THE WOODSHOP MAINTENANCE HANDBOOK

SAL MACCARONE

BETTERWAY BOOKS

CINCINNATI, OHIO

Disclaimer

To prevent accidents, keep safety in mind while you work. Use the safety guards installed on power equipment; they are for your protection. When working on power equipment, keep fingers away from saw blades, wear safety goggles to prevent injuries from flying wood chips and sawdust, wear headphones to protect your hearing.

Tune Up Your Tools: The Woodshop Maintenance Handbook. Copyright © 1996 by Sal Maccarone. Printed and bound in the United States of America. All rights reserved. No part of this book may be reproduced in any form or by any electronic or mechanical means including information storage and retrieval systems without permission in writing from the publisher, except by a reviewer, who may quote brief passages in a review. Published by Betterway Books, an imprint of F&W Publications, Inc., 1507 Dana Avenue, Cincinnati, Ohio 45207. (800) 289-0963. First edition.

Other fine Betterway Books are available from your local bookstore or direct from the publisher.

00 99 98 97 96   5 4 3 2 1

Library of Congress Cataloging-in-Publication Data

Maccarone, Sal.
    Tune up your tools : the woodshop maintenance handbook / by Sal Maccarone.
        p.   cm.
        Includes index.
        ISBN 1-55870-409-4 (pbk.)
        1. Woodworking tools—Maintenance and repair. 2. Sharpening of tools. I. Title.
TT186.M33 1996
621.9′0028′8—dc20   96-968
                                                       CIP

Editor: R. Adam Blake
Production editor: Bruce E. Stoker
Cover and Interior designer: Brian Roeth
Cover photography: Pamela Monfort Braun/Bronze Photography
Interior photography: David Thiel
Computer Illustrations: Bob Shreve
Special thanks to Aufdemkampe Hardware, 2000 Central Parkway, Cincinnati, Ohio 45214, for the products used in the photography for the book.

Betterway Books are available for sales promotions, premiums and fund-raising use. Special editions or book excerpts can also be created to specification. For details contact: Special Sales Manager, F&W Publications, 1507 Dana Avenue, Cincinnati, Ohio 45207.

Dedication

To my sister Donna S. Nowland with love.

METRIC CONVERSION CHART		
TO CONVERT	**TO**	**MULTIPLY BY**
Inches	Centimeters	2.54
Centimeters	Inches	0.4
Feet	Centimeters	30.5
Centimeters	Feet	0.03
Yards	Meters	0.9
Meters	Yards	1.1
Sq. Inches	Sq. Centimeters	6.45
Sq. Centimeters	Sq. Inches	0.16
Sq. Feet	Sq. Meters	0.09
Sq. Meters	Sq. Feet	10.8
Sq. Yards	Sq. Meters	0.8
Sq. Meters	Sq. Yards	1.2
Pounds	Kilograms	0.45
Kilograms	Pounds	2.2
Ounces	Grams	28.4
Grams	Ounces	0.04

About the Author

Built of Honduran mahogany, walnut and brass, this CEO's inner-office is part of an 11,000 square feet corporate headquarters in San Francisco. The woodwork for the entire headquarters was designed and built by Sal Maccarone (seated).

In a class of his own, Sal Maccarone is both a journeyman cabinetmaker and a master woodwork designer/craftsman. With college degrees in both art and sculpture from San Jose State University, he has owned and operated his own company, Woodwork Design, since 1972. Working his way through the baccalaureate years while completing a four-year cabinetmaker's apprenticeship, he graduated with honors the same year he became a journeyman in 1971. During his postgraduate years at the university, Sal also had the unique opportunity of serving an apprenticeship to an international multimedia sculptor.

During his twenty-four years in business, Sal has the privilege of completing commission after commission in both the private and business worlds. His work can be viewed in hotels and other public spaces all over the country. Calling his unique style of woodwork "utilitarian art," he has always managed to blend his sculpture into the design of the functional.

Acknowledgments

It is extremely hard to acknowledge everyone who has influenced your life leading up to and during the writing of a book. There are so many positive influences along the way which do contribute to the knowledge necessary for grasping any subject. Where this book is concerned, I would like to mention just a few people who helped me through the process, but there are several others who will always hold a special place in my thoughts.

I would like to thank my friend and editor, Adam Blake, for both giving me this opportunity and encouraging me every step of the way. Sharon, my best friend and wife of twenty-five years, is a very special and selfless lady who not only gave up a lot of evenings and weekends, but did so believing in my work for this book. My son, Andy, who helped me with all of the conceptual photography, gave his personal time without question. My son, Sam, who is in los Angeles becoming an actor, encouraged me with his ability to sacrifice and his dedication to such a competitive field. My father, Mr. C.A. Maccarone, who has always been there for me, is the whole reason that I became interested in woodworking as a little boy.

Thanks to all of you.
Sal Maccarone

Table of Contents

Introduction

Any tool is basically an extension of the person that uses it. They are the vehicles to our expression as artists, trade and craft persons. With that in mind, it only stands to reason that the more knowledge we can acquire about our tools, the better we can express ourselves. Just like anything else we need to build upon a firm foundation. A mental foundation which is made to include a good understanding of the tools which bring us to realize our goals. Armed with this information we can not only save money by being efficient, but we can do a better job with what is at our disposal.

As a mill cabinet and art student in the late 1960s, I was intrigued with the versatility of the power tools, especially the stationary ones. After college, I began my business in 1972 with a good knowledge of the two power tools that I owned. I did not know it then, but at the time it was one of the things that meant the difference between my failure or success. Now, some twenty-four years and five thousand plus projects later, I find the need to share this attitude with whoever might feel benefitted by it. With this book I would like to focus on the principles, ongoing adjustments, and maintenance of each power tool, stationary and hand-held, most commonly found in the woodshop.

I consider these to be as follows: table saw, band saw, radial arm saw, lathe, surface planer, jointer, shaper, spindle sander, drill press, router, saber saw, pad sanders, biscuit jointer, drill motors, and the hand held circular saw.

During my career in business as a furniture maker and sculptor, I have found it necessary to get "just a little more" from each of my tools. In other words, I keep my tools well maintained and adjusted, thereby realizing the full potential. I feel that it saves a lot of time and money just to be aware of a tool's capability in terms of adjustment. This book is designed to give an experienced explanation of each of the tools mentioned above. If only to gain an understanding of how things work, or maybe to acquire some know-how for that special home improvement project, this information should be helpful to all.

For the purpose of this book, I would like to give an overview of all woodworking tools with an emphasis on safety. Each operation that we perform must be very carefully thought out on well maintained and adjusted equipment. I never turn on the tool until first thinking about what might go wrong with the operation I am about to perform. I always go through a quick mental checklist of all things pertaining to that tool.

This also helps to keep my respect for that tool each time I use it.

There are specific safety concerns with each tool category which must be learned and absorbed before that tool is operated for the first time. Such things as tool rotation, potential kickbacks, tolerances, feed direction, and proper use of guards are all paramount concerns. Before these can be considered there is a host of other, more underlying rules that should always be adhered to when operating any machine. Some of these underlying safety concepts which apply to all power tools and that should always be kept in mind would have to include:

- Never operate a power tool if you are under the influence of medication or alcohol.
- Never operate a power tool if you are tired or preoccupied with other thoughts.
- Never operate a power tool when there is overbearing noise or other distractions present in the room.
- Be sure that all electrical connections are clean and that circuits are not overloaded.
- Be sure that all blades, bits, sanding belts and cutters are sound and not over-fatigued.

Regarding the performance of all tools, they must be maintained well, especially the bigger stationary tools. These are the ones which have the most horsepower and potential for mishap. Stationary is the key word here. Be it on wood or concrete each of these tools should be anchored to the floor. You do not need the added worry of trying to foresee an accident caused by the tool walking away, and there are many technical flaws that might occur due to vibration. Try and check all moving parts often, including the drive belts. I do this while applying lubricant every so many working hours depending upon the tool. As per this manual,

it does not hurt to have a simple maintenance schedule on a specific calendar which will only help add to the life of the tool.

Understand the principles of each tool that you operate. The anatomy, which includes all of the moving parts, the horsepower, and the speed at which the tool is operating, along with all other facts and specifications. Study information supplied with the tool as well as any other basic text that you can find. With this type of technical knowledge, you can have a well-maintained body of tools which can only add to your proficiency

and safety.

It makes good business sense to try and realize that best return that we can on our investments. Needless to say, our tools are big investments. When it is necessary to purchase a new tool, I always try to buy the best quality that I can afford at the time, and then maintain it well. In this same manner I was able to build my shop slowly as space and money allowed while working with good, well-maintained equipment all along the way.

CHAPTER ONE

The Table Saw

The table saw, or variety saw as it is lovingly called by some, is a most impressive tool. A basic piece of machinery, it is designed to afford us the ability to make straight, accurate cuts every time—if it's properly maintained. Having had to produce laborious cuts by hand in the field, I never take my table saw for granted when I get back to the shop, realizing all of the time it saves me every day, not to mention all the creative doors it opens. With all of this in mind, there should be a basic respect and devotion to maintenance, as with all power tools. The difference between an amateur and a professional, in my mind, is the willingness to understand why the tool does what it does, and then take the time to care for it.

This versatile tool is basically a motor-driven arbor connected by a framework to a table; the table remains in a fixed horizontal position and the arbor tilts. The size of the saw is determined by the diameter

Every table saw has depth and angle adjustments. This would be a typical arrangement: The depth adjustment is in the front (left) and the angle adjustment is on the side (right).

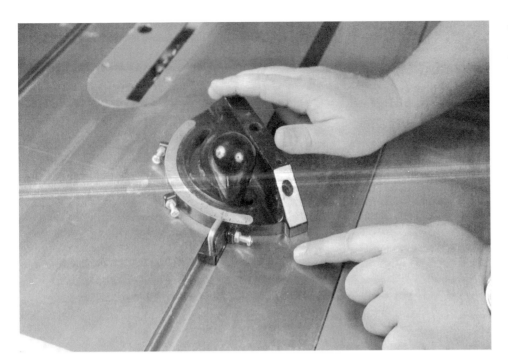

All factory supplied miter gauges have a means to set the angle. It is critical these gauges be kept in perfect adjustment to ensure perfect angle cuts, whatever they might be. Note the three adjustable screw-type angle stops.

Most rip fences have these two adjustments: a means to move the fence left or right and a lock to clamp the fence in place once it is set the proper distance from the blade.

of the blade that is recommended for use (10″ is the most common size found in the shop). The saw blade works in conjunction with either a rip fence or a miter gauge in normal operation. There are means to set the blade depth and angle (see figure at left). There is also an angle adjustment on the miter gauge that slides in the slots milled into the table top (see top figure). The fence has an incremental lateral adjustment and a lock to be used once it has been set the desired distance from the blade (see bottom figure).

Many makes and models are available in today's expanding market. They are all the same conceptually, and require basically the same care and adjustments. Some things to consider when shopping for a table saw would be size, power and capacity. I separate table saws into two categories; the direct drive (or contractor's type) and the belt-driven, more stationary, cabinet shop type (see figure at right). Depending on your particular application, both types are true time-savers and can be exceedingly accurate within their own limitations. In my mind, what is more important than the size and capabilities of the saw is the craftsperson who is operating it. The well focused, maintenance-minded operator of a less impressive machine can produce better products than the lax or casual operator of the world's best machine.

SAFETY RULES

There are underlying safety concerns that we must always bear in mind. In addition to those we must also be in tune with each specific tool's set of cardinal rules. Never lose respect for the fact that this machine is designed primarily to cut wood. It is a wonderful tool, but unfortunately it will never be able to distinguish between wood and our fragile bodies. It is the operator's responsibility to decide what is passed through the blade.

Common sense tells us that a well adjusted and clean tool in a clutter-free environment will contribute to safety. Sharp blades or cutters will certainly add to our proficiency and safety by diminishing the possibilities of binding or kickback. I have made it a habit never to stand directly behind the cutters: To avoid kickback I will stand to one side or the other, depending upon the operation at hand.

One very basic rule is to use the guard provided with the saw. Some operations require the removal of that guard, and we should always be aware of the increased danger

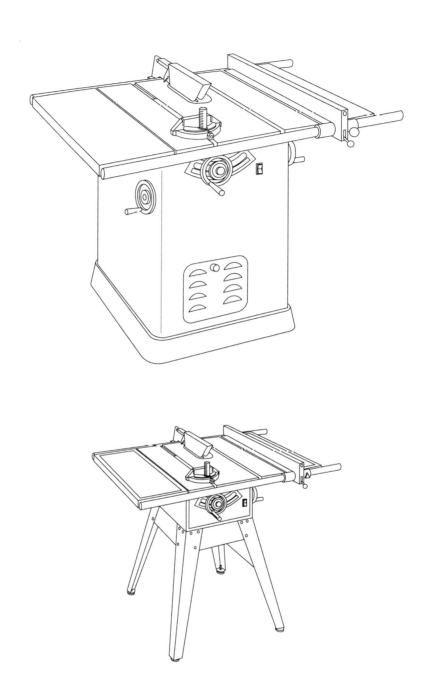

There are basically two categories of table saw: the more stationary, solid base, belt-driven cabinet shop type and the portable, direct drive contractor's, or bench top, type. The saws are the same in principle, but the cabinet shop type usually will deliver more power.

Table Saw
Maintenance Schedule

Serial Number:

Date of Purchase:

Parts to be changed (yearly):   Belts

Parts to be aligned (5 hours):   Fence, Miter gage, Splitter, Guard, Anti-kickback pawls, Motor and arbor pulleys

Parts to be oiled (10 hours):   Trunnion gear, worm gear, Arbor gear, Fence travel gear

Parts to be waxed (1-2 hours):   Table top, Fence, Miter gage

Date	Hours of Operation	Maintenance Notes

For longevity and accuracy's sake it is always a good idea to keep a maintenance schedule like this one for every power tool. Note that the top of the sheet contains all of the information needed to properly maintain the tool.

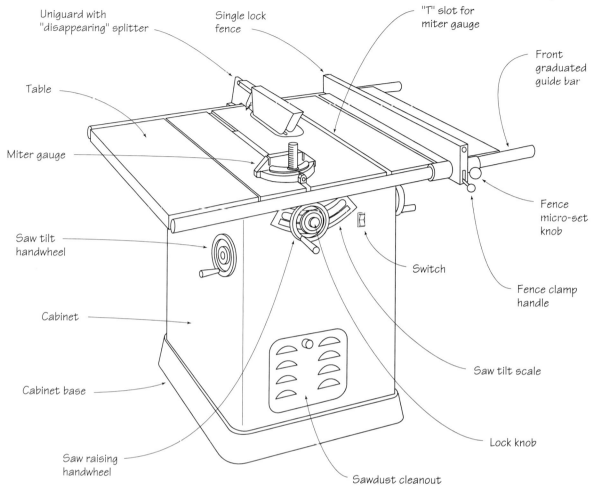

Uniguard with "disappearing" splitter

Single lock fence

"T" slot for miter gauge

Front graduated guide bar

Table

Miter gauge

Saw tilt handwheel

Cabinet

Cabinet base

Saw raising handwheel

Sawdust cleanout

Switch

Fence micro-set knob

Fence clamp handle

Saw tilt scale

Lock knob

It is important to know the moving parts of your particular table saw and then note them on your maintenance schedule for cleaning and oiling. This is the typical anatomy of the table saw.

Safety Rules

- Make sure the fence is locked in place after setting the width.
- Always keep the work firmly down on the table while it passes the blade.
- Keep the work riding against the fence throughout the operation.
- Do not have excessive overhang of the work beyond blade.
- Do not feed the material faster than the saw will accept.
- Avoid using wet lumber, as it can bind, kickback, and cause rusting.
- Avoid using warped or twisted wood as it can cause kickback and inaccurate cuts.
- Always use a pushstick when the fence is set close to the blade.
- Never stand in line with the blade.
- Always unplug the saw when changing the blades.
- Never reach over the blade or cutter.
- Always wear eye protection.

potential. Read and digest all of the information provided with the saw. Each saw is a little different in terms of design. The fence, which way the blade tilts, the size of the table and the horsepower are just some of the variables that should be paid attention to.

I keep a copy of the checklist printed at the end of this chapter tacked up by my saw. A quick rundown before each operation increases proficiency and helps to remind me of any particular safety concerns that may be associated with that operation. It's a good insurance policy!

ASSEMBLY AND INSTALLATION

Before the table saw can be operated it must be properly assembled and installed. Many saws are pre-assembled at the factory or retailer where they are purchased. Even these should be scrutinized with a fine-tooth comb. Make yourself familiar with the specific anatomy of your saw. Check each part against the schematic provided in the owner's manual and make sure that everything is tight. It is a good idea to relubricate all moving parts at this time.

MAINTENANCE SCHEDULE

Make yourself a maintenance schedule noting the date of purchase and the parts to be oiled, greased or changed (pagee 11). This chart should be tacked up in some obvious place where it will not be lost or forgotten. I like to run my maintenance schedules according to actual hours of usage, with the exception of the belts. Being made of rubber, these drive belts are prone to deterioration; I change my belts once a year just to be safe. Where the table saw is concerned, I clean and lubricate all moving parts after each ten hours of actual use (see figure at left). While doing this I also check to see if anything needs to be tightened or adjusted. It is a good idea to note these adjustments, and any parts that are showing signs of wear, on your maintenance schedule along with the date.

SAW LOCATION

Location and placement of the table saw in a shop should be well thought out. I liken this to cooking and the kitchen, where every tool

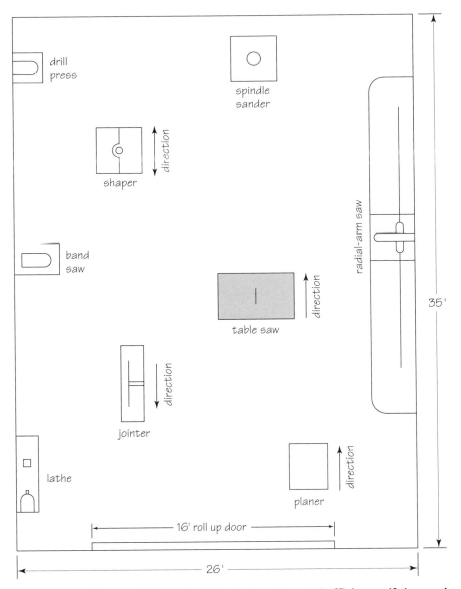

Placement of the saw is important for both safety and efficiency. If the work space allows, this would be the ideal arrangement. Note how the saw is placed central to all of the other tools.

is placed into what is known as a "golden triangle." The table saw should be central to all of the other tools (see figure at right). It requires the most floor space and is also the most important tool in any cabinet or furniture shop. The minimum space required is ten feet behind and in front of the blade, with six feet to either side of the blade. If more room is available, so much the better.

Once the location is determined, the saw should be mounted to the floor for stability. Most accidents—and a lot of inaccuracies—occur due to the saw "walking" across the floor while making a cut. Even portable table saws should be clamped or somehow temporarily fastened while in use (above). When you have a wooden floor, installation is easy; a concrete or masonry floor is a little different situation. In this case I would level and mount a piece of ¾" plywood, on

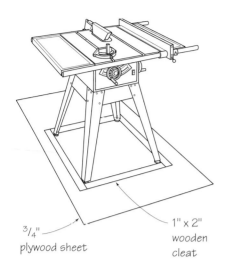

³/₄"
plywood sheet

1" x 2"
wooden
cleat

Even the portable table saw should be secured if possible. This is an example of one quick and easy means by which this may be done. The plywood sheet extends in front of the machine so that the weight of the operator holds it down. The sheet can be stored while the machine is not in use.

which the saw will fit, to the floor for a permanent installation. Otherwise, expandable anchors can be installed directly into the floor and the saw can be anchored to these while in use.

Whether the saw is portable or mounted permanently, it is a good idea to paint a line around the area of operation on the floor (see figure at top right on page 14). While the saw is in use this area should be kept clear of all obstructions, including people not directly involved in the operation. This will help to minimize distractions, and is in the safety interests of every one in the room.

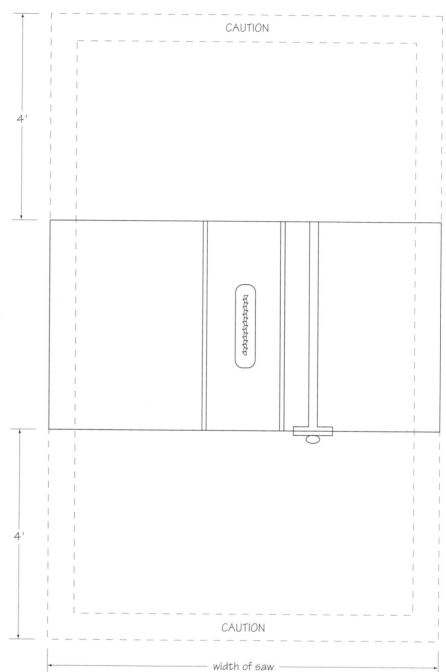

CAUTION

4'

4'

CAUTION

width of saw

The caution line reminds both operator and others in the room not to stand in "the line of fire" while the saw is in use. It will also keep the space from becoming cluttered when the saw is not in use.

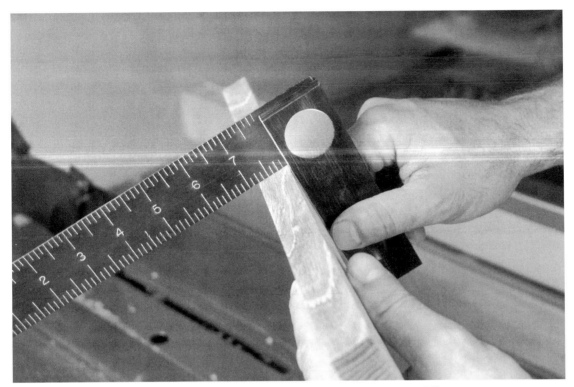

It is a good practice to check a piece of scrap with a square once in a while at random. Even a minor deviation from square can play havoc with your project once assembly has begun.

VACUUMS AND DUST COLLECTORS

For permanent installation of an enclosed-base saw, some sort of dust collection system should be considered. A multitude of relatively inexpensive options can handle this chore. The bottom line is to exhaust the dust away from the motor and moving parts each time the saw is used. The enclosed base is nice in terms of stability, but should never be allowed to fill with sawdust. All enclosed-base saws provide a port somewhere at the bottom to attach the exhausting tool: If a formal dust collector is too expensive, a simple shop-vac with the proper adaptor can be used. The shop-vac can be wired directly into the switch of the saw so that it becomes operational each time the saw is turned on.

ADJUSTMENT AND ALIGNMENT

All table saws are made of parts that are bolted and screwed together. These parts can loosen and slip due to the vibration of use. If not checked regularly this will begin to manifest itself as inaccuracies in the work. It is a good idea to make some occasional spot checks for these inaccuracies along the way (above).

There is a multitude of table saw makes and models which are each a little different. Methods of adjustment will differ from saw to saw, but the basic relationships of the parts to each other all remain the same. Carefully study the owner's manual for your particular saw; it will explain how these basic adjustments are made.

Adjustments

1. How the fence is moved and locked.
2. How the miter gauge is set and locked.
3. Which angles have preset stops on the miter gauge and how to adjust them.
4. How to raise and lower the blade.
5. How to tilt the blade and lock it at the desired angle.
6. How to adjust the 90° stop for the blade.

ALIGNMENT

Some important relationships hold true for every table saw. First, the rip fence, blade or cutter, and the miter gauge slots in the table must all be parallel. Second, the rip fence and miter gauge must be at 90° to the table. Third, the throat plate should be flush with the table top (see figures at right).

Table Top

The table top itself should be perfectly flat, or none of this will work. I always check the table with a long straight edge before beginning the alignment process (page 17 top).

Once the table has been confirmed to be flat, I make sure that the blade is parallel to the miter gauge slots in the table. This is done by raising the blade all the way and placing a three-foot ruler against it (page 17 middle). Make sure that the ruler is lying flat against the blade—between the teeth if possible. Next, I measure from both the back and the front of the ruler to either slot in the table (page 17 bottom). If they are not parallel, refer to your owner's manual for the means to correct this on your saw. All other alignment is based on this relationship, so this must be correct.

At this point I check that the rip fence is parallel to the miter gauge slots, and consequently the blade. This can be done by placing a dimensioned stick into one of the slots in the table (page 18 top); move the fence to within a few inches of the stick and lock it in place.

The space between the stick and the fence should be the same both back and front (page 18 bottom); if not, this could cause binding or

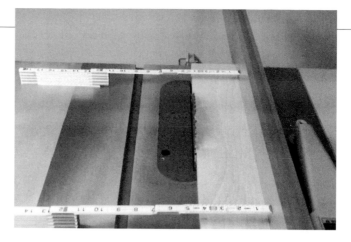

Three important relationships are present in every table saw. First and foremost, the table slots, blade and fence must be parallel.

The second important relationship has to do with the rip fence and miter gauge head: They must be at 90° to the table top. Check them with a square as shown.

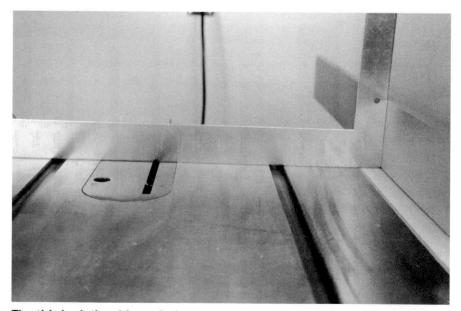

The third relationship typical to every table saw involves the throat plate: This plate must be flush to the table top. All three relationships should be checked periodically.

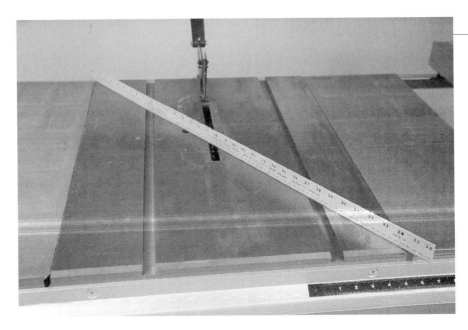

The table top must be flat! Before you purchase a used saw or try to make any of the adjustments for the first time, this must be verified. This is done by placing a straight edge diagonally across the top both ways.

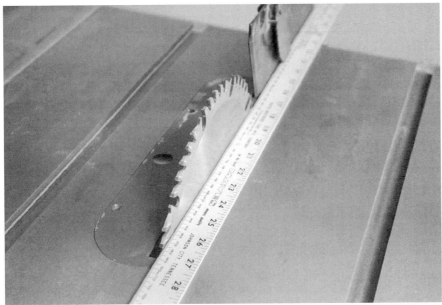

To check the alignment of the blade to the table there are two steps. First place a ruler between the teeth of the raised blade as shown in this photo.

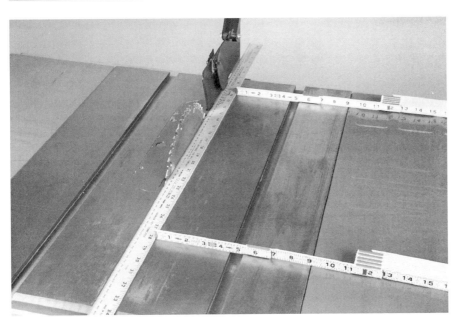

Once the ruler is in place, measure from the edge (both front and back) of the table to either miter gauge slot. The measurements should be equal.

To check the alignment of the fence to the miter gauge table slots, place a dimensioned piece of wood into one of the slots in the table as shown.

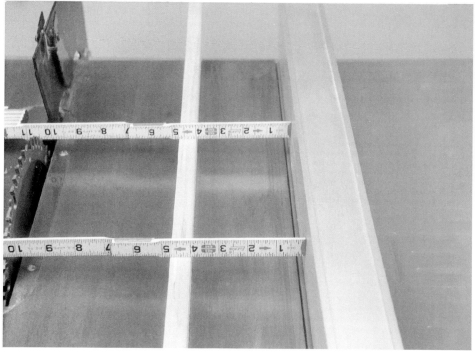

Once the dimensioned piece is placed securely in the slot closest to the fence, measure from each end of the stick to the fence. The measurements should be equal for proper alignment.

burning of the cut edge. Every fence and fence guide system has a means to correct this problem.

Next, I run a quick check with a square to see if the fence and miter gauge head both are perpendicular to the table top (page 19 top). If the fence tracking system is installed correctly this should not be a problem. If the miter gauge is not perpendicular I check that the track is clear and that the bottom of the slide is clean. If these two things do not pan out, the tool may be bent. I might add that I have encountered this problem only once in my long career. Along with this operation, I also check the relationship of the miter gauge to the blade with the square. Once verified, the 90° stop on the gauge should be adjusted and set.

The Throat

The throat plate must be flush with the table top. This is checked by placing a square or straight edge across the table and plate (page 19 bottom). Some manufacturers provide a screw-type adjustment either on the plate or in the table where the plate is inserted. If the plate is designed to fit flush without adjustment and does not, the culprit may be sawdust buildup. Adjustable plate or not, the sawdust should be cleaned out of this area each time the blade is changed. A plate that is not flush can cause a board to "snag" either before or after it has entered the blade.

The Splitter

The splitter, which is usually part of the guard assembly, is located directly behind the blade. The space in the board that is removed

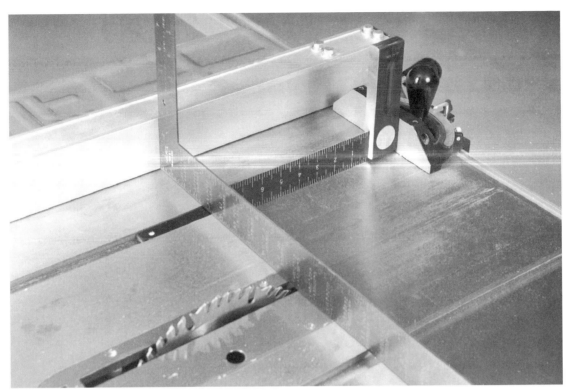

To check that the fence and miter gauge are perpendicular to the table top, lay a true square against each as shown. This should be checked periodically as part of your maintenance schedule.

If the throat plate is not flush with the table top it could cause a snag. To check this, first clean around the plate slot thoroughly. Once the plate is back in place, lay a square or straight edge over each end of the plate as shown.

by the saw blade is called a "kerf" (page 20 top). The splitter is used to keep the saw-kerf open, which keeps the wood from binding behind the blade. To check this alignment I raise the blade to maximum height and place the three-foot ruler on each side of the blade and splitter, making sure that the ruler is against the blade and not touching the teeth (middle figure at right). If the ruler touches the splitter on either side, it is out of alignment. I then loosen the connecting bolts and realign the splitter. Once re-tightened, I check again with the ruler.

The Blades

There could not be a chapter about table saw maintenance without some mention of the blades. This is not a book about tool operation, so I will not get into the many types of blades that are available. The one thing that does hold true for all blades to operate efficiently is that they must be sharp. Besides being dangerous, a dull blade can cause some of the same symptoms as misalignment. As a matter of fact, a dull blade can cause misalignment to occur.

I do not recommend that blades be sharpened at home, unless one has the specific equipment to do this. Sharpening saw blades is a job for professionals who do have the proper equipment. Most professional sharpeners are quite reasonable with their rates, but it does pay to shop around. In large metropolitan areas there are even services that include pickup and delivery of blades. I do recommend that the blades be cleaned by the operator between sharpenings; this can be done with fine steel wool and

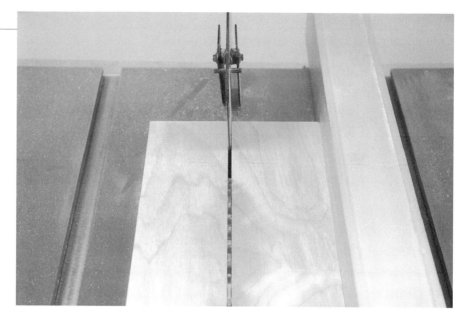

The saw-kerf is defined as the area that has been removed by the blade. Note how the kerf passes around the splitter without touching either side.

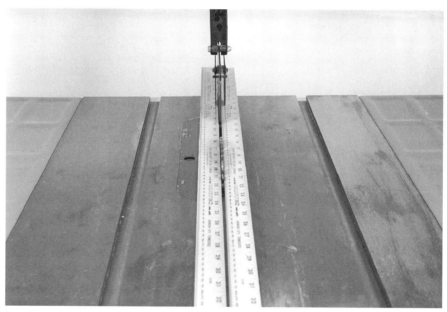

To align the splitter, place a ruler between the teeth on each side of the blade and along the splitter. If properly adjusted, neither ruler should touch the splitter.

The blade should be cleaned periodically between sharpenings to remove any pitch or tar. This should be done with fine (0000) steel wool and lacquer thinner. Dry the blade well and store it properly.

lacquer thinner. Make sure to dry the blade well after cleaning, then store it in a safe place where it will not get dropped, banged or otherwise damaged.

The Arbor Assembly

Depending on your saw type you will have either a motor pulley to arbor pulley arrangement or a motor arbor assembly (direct drive). If your saw is the more stationary pulley type, it is necessary to check the pulley alignment. If alignment is needed this will require adjustment of the motor via the mounts. The pulleys themselves should be true. The reasoning here is to avoid unnecessary stress on the motor or arbor bearings.

If the bearings in the arbor are bad due to wear, they need to be replaced. This will become evident by the clicking noise produced by bad bearings. If you hear this unusual noise, check—with the tool unplugged—to see if there is any play in the saw blade that is mounted to the arbor: There should be no play whatsoever. If replacement is needed, check your owner's manual parts list and replacement instructions. The saw should not be used until these bearings have been replaced.

The arbor assembly consists of a threaded shaft with a fixed flange, a washer and a nut (above right). If the fixed flange is not true or has runout, the arbor should be replaced. This would be evident while observing the blade as it comes to a stop after the machine has been turned off. If the blade wobbles even slightly, there is a problem, but before replacing the arbor it is a good idea to check this again with another blade. If the

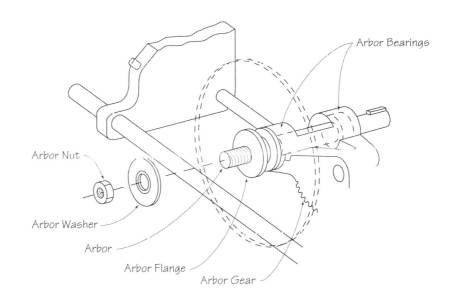

This is a typical arbor assembly diagram. Each manufacturer's arbor is a little different, but basic principles apply.

The arbor washer should be flat! If it is not flat and free of burrs, a simple honing on a flat surface in order. Use a 400 to 600 grit wet and dry paper with a light oil as the cutting agent.

second blade runs true, the first blade is probably warped and should be discarded. The arbor washer distributes the force of the nut and must also be flat and free of bumps. This washer should be worked over with a flat sharpening stone if there is any doubt.

CLEANING AND WAXING

Once all of the adjustments are done, and as part of the ongoing maintenance schedule, the tool should be cleaned and waxed. I use light oil lubricant and fine steel wool to clean the table top. After the top has been wiped clean, I apply caruba paste floor wax, which comes in stick form for canning purposes. I also apply this wax to the faces of both the rip fence and miter gauge. This will make the work glide across all surfaces, and consequently reduces burning and chattering. The surfaces look good too!

Table Saw Troubleshooting at a Glance

1. Cut edge is not square

PROBLEM	SOLUTION
Blade is not square with table	Bring blade to full depth of cut, check with a square, adjust to 90° and reset indicator to 0°

2. Sawtooth marks on cut edge

PROBLEM	SOLUTION
Dull or bad blade	Sharpen or replace blade
Poor fence alignment	Check that fence is not binding on the back side of the blade; readjust fence
Arbor alignment	Adjust alignment of the arbor to the table and fence

3. Finished parts narrower than expected or not parallel

PROBLEM	SOLUTION
Incremental setting on fence not accurate	Measure from blade to the fence and reset fence
Fence not parallel to blade and table	Measure from front and back of blade to fence and adjust fence; fence should also be parallel to miter gauge slot

4. Kickback; blade bogs down or burns work

PROBLEM	SOLUTION
Dull, dirty or incorrect blade	Check blade for residue buildup; blade in use is correct for applications
Incorrect alignment of fence to blade	Realign fence; make sure that the antikickback fingers are adjusted properly

5. Work binds between fence and blade or moves away from fence

PROBLEM	SOLUTION
Incorrect alignment of fence to blade	Realign fence; make sure fence tracking system and fence lock are tight

6. Work binds behind the saw blade

PROBLEM	SOLUTION
Incorrect splitter alignment	Loosen nuts and realign splitter
Throat plate not flush with table top	Adjust plate to flush

7. Miter gauge sticks on table or in slots

PROBLEM	SOLUTION
Gauge or table slots damaged or not clean	Clean and wax miter gauge and table; check for burrs in gauge bar and table slots

8. Work jams between blade and miter gauge

PROBLEM	SOLUTION
Miter gauge square to slots but not blade	Adjust arbor alignment per owner's manual
Bad bearings or warped blade	Replace bearings or blade

9. Chattering on moulded edges or dadoes

PROBLEM	SOLUTION
Dull or misaligned cutters	Have cutters sharpened; check alignment of cutters
Dirty or sticky table	Clean and wax table

10. Blade binds in saw-kerf

PROBLEM	SOLUTION
Dull blade	Sharpen or replace blade
Splitter not aligned properly	Align splitter per number 6; make sure splitter is not bent

Table Saw

ALL OPERATIONS:
✔ Blade tightened on arbor
✔ Blade set ½″ above stock and locked
✔ Arbor tilt lock secured
✔ Throat plate in place and flush
✔ Table top waxed
✔ No obstructions around saw
✔ Safety glasses on

RIPPING OPERATIONS:
✔ Rip fence parallel to blade
✔ Rip fence perpendicular to table
✔ Rip fence locked
✔ Rip fence waxed

CROSSCUTTING OPERATIONS:
✔ Miter gauge set and locked
✔ Gauge slots free of dust and waxed
✔ Gauge bar waxed

CHAPTER TWO

Radial Arm Saw

What a power shop this is! Next to the table saw, this has got to be the most versatile tool in the wood shop. An excellent crosscut saw, this tool can also be used as a drill, shaper, jointer, sander, router or wood lathe. This should bring to mind the obvious need for ongoing maintenance and adjustment. In order to stay within the context of this manual, I will not elaborate on the many diverse uses of this piece of equipment. As always, I recommend that you read and absorb all you can regarding the potential of any tool that you own or operate.

The radial arm saw is primarily used for accurate crosscutting of all kinds, including compound miters, dadoes, rabbets and straight cuts. Whereas the table saw is best suited for ripping operations, the radial saw can also be adjusted to rip. With that exception, all of the cutting is done with the work held in a fixed position on the table and the cutter assembly moved across the work.

The overarm (or track), which holds the yoke, motor and blade, will rotate to the left and right. This gives the ability to do crosscut miters.

All of the cutting is done from above. The blade is not hidden below the work as with the table saw.

RADIAL ARM SAW ANATOMY

One of the most common saws seen in the shop and on construction sites is the radial arm saw. Basically this tool can be described as a pivotal motor unit that moves back and forth under a pivotal overarm. This whole assembly can be made to move up or down via the depth adjustment. The blade or cutter is attached to the arbor which extends directly from the motor. The size of the blade recommended by the manufacturer determines the size of the saw; the most common sizes for home and shop use are the 10" and 12" models. The entire assembly is mounted to a stand or workbench at a comfortable height. The saw bench is discussed in the assembly and installation section of this chapter.

There are three main functions to this tool. These same functions are used for setting up any of the many operations that it is capable of. The overarm or track will rotate 180° (page 24). The yoke, which holds the motor will rotate 360° (top right). The motor unit, which holds the blade, will tilt or rotate 90° in either direction (bottom right). This gives the tool compound capabilities for which there are no substitutes.

RADIAL ARM SAW SAFETY

Beyond our usual underlying safety concerns, this saw does have its own particular set of rules. Again, a clean, well oiled and maintained tool will help to dimin-

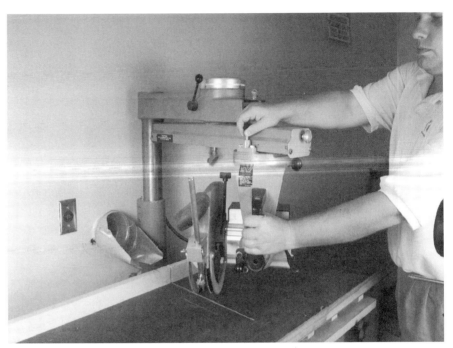

The yoke, which holds the motor, can swivel 360° under the overarm. This gives the ability to rip cut, with the material being pushed along the fence.

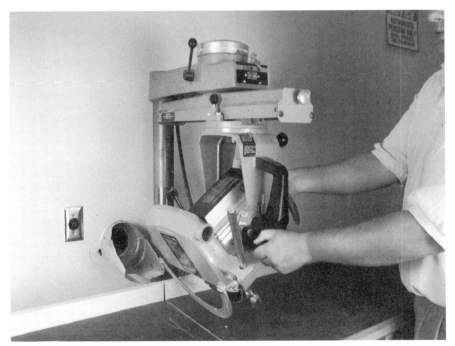

The motor and arbor can swivel 360° within the yoke. Among other things, this affords the ability to bevel or compound crosscut.

ish problems with the machine itself. The clutter-free floor and saw bench is also common sense in terms of avoiding senseless accidents.

It is an absolute must that the guard provided with the saw is mounted at all times (above). Unlike the table saw, the blade would be 100 percent exposed without this guard. The exhaust port for sawdust is also housed within the guard, which is yet another reason not to remove it. Because the saw

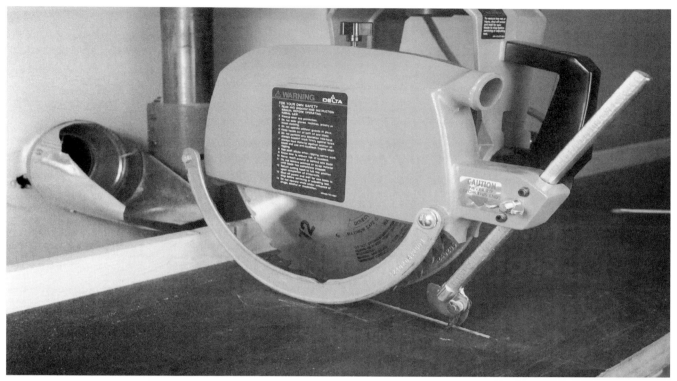

The guard, which holds the antikickback device, must be mounted at all times when a blade is in use. Note that the blade would be totally exposed without the guard.

is located at waist height and the dust is prone to collect on the bench, it is very important that the guard port be connected to an exhaust system. This should be done for health and safety, as well as efficiency, reasons.

Read your manual to gain an understanding of all locks and tool principles. I keep a copy of the checklist printed at the end of this chapter tacked up on the wall. The checklist reminds me of the particular safety concerns associated with this saw.

Safety Rules

- Do not pull the blade through the work faster than it will cut.
- Make sure that the work is supported well on both sides of the blade.
- Make sure that all pivotal part clamps are locked before operating.
- Keep the work firmly against the fence while cutting.
- Set the blade ⅛″ below the table surface during normal operation.
- Always unplug the tool when making adjustments or changing the blades.
- Never stand directly in front of the blade when the tool is in operation.
- Always make sure that the guard and exhaust system are in place and tightened down.
- Never raise or lower the blade when the saw is on.
- Never operate the tool without safety glasses.

RADIAL ARM SAW ASSEMBLY AND INSTALLATION

Before the saw can be operated it must be properly assembled and installed. Most radial saws are assembled at the factory. If a stand is purchased it will most likely come in a box to be assembled, which is simply a matter of following instructions. Even if assembled, the saw itself should be checked against the schematic. Each part should be scrutinized and tightened if necessary. This will familiarize you with the saw's anatomy (top right).

If you purchase a base or stand for your saw it will most likely have to be extended. Because of the nature of this tool, it is best to have as long a support as possible on both sides of the blade (bottom right). If an additional bench is not possible, there should be some sort of portable "dead man"-type support on each side to carry the weight of long pieces of stock.

RADIAL ARM SAW MAINTENANCE

Make yourself a maintenance schedule similar to the one used for the table saw. This schedule should note the date of purchase, serial number, and any parts to be oiled or greased (page 28). The radial arm saw is a direct-drive tool; therefore there are no belts to change. The schedule should also include the bench and fixed stop, which have become part of the tool. The bench should be level, flat, and perpendicular to the blade during normal use. The stop should be perfectly straight, and 90° to the blade when the overarm is set at 0°.

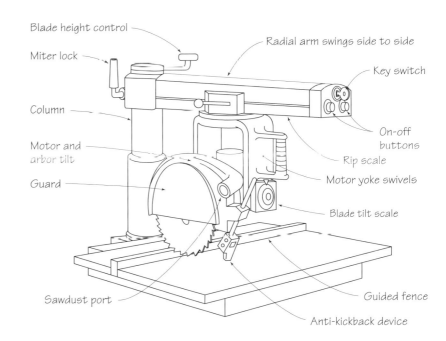

Regardless of manufacturer, this would be a typical radial saw anatomy.

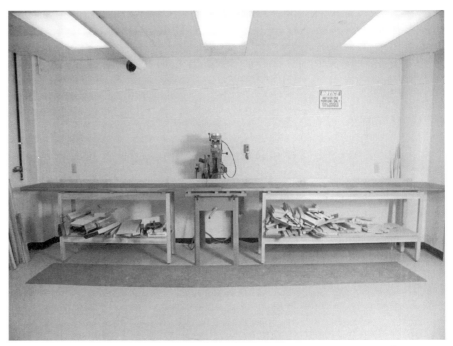

The radial saw bench should extend on both sides of the blade as far as possible. Material should be supported on each side of the cut.

Radial Arm Saw
Maintenance Schedule

Serial Number:

Date of Purchase:

Parts to be aligned (3 hours):   Overarm, motor, yoke, guard angle indicator scales, roller bearings, table top, fence, adjustment stops

Parts to be oiled (5 hours):   Roller bearings, all pivotal points, column

Parts to be waxed (1-2 hours):   Table top, fence

Date	Hours of Operation	Maintenance Notes

It is wise to keep a maintenance schedule for your records. Note that the date of purchase, serial number, and all maintenance information is listed.

With the radial saw, I clean and lubricate all moving parts after each five hours of use. Because this saw is "above board" and out in the open, it is more prone to collecting dirt and dust within the moving parts than, say, the more enclosed table saw. I always note the date the saw is cleaned, oiled or adjusted on my maintenance schedule. This accurate schedule keeps me "in tune" with my saw, and also becomes an impressive feature if I ever decide to sell the tool in an effort to upgrade.

RADIAL ARM SAW LOCATION

For permanent installation in a cabinet shop, the radial arm saw should be placed in the center of the longest wall available (see figure top right). Remembering the "golden triangle," this saw should also be as close to the table saw as possible. When placed this way the saw and bench can be mounted directly to the wall and floor for ultimate stability. Incidentally, the end of this long, stable bench is an ideal place to mount a flush-type woodworker's vise.

If in the field or a temporary location, the saw base should still be stabilized. This can be done by making a stabilization plate if working on concrete (see top figure page 30); if you are working on a wooden floor, the base can be mounted directly to the floor with screws and washers. Remember, this is a stationary power tool and should never be allowed to vibrate across the floor.

Realizing that for permanent installation the saw and accompanying bench will take up the whole wall, the caution line should only

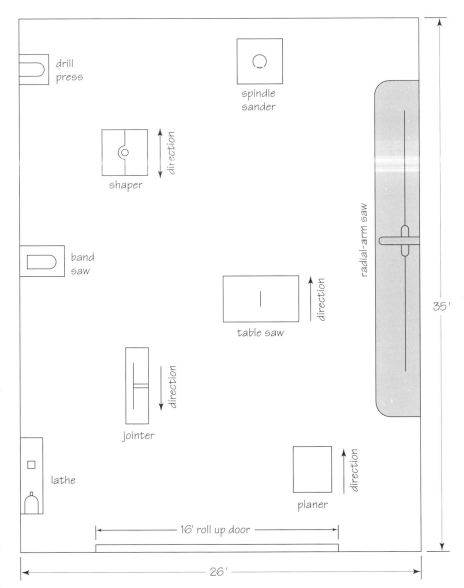

For permanent installation it is best to place the radial saw on the longest wall in the shop that is closest to the table saw.

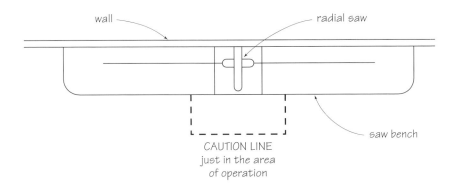

When the saw is mounted on a permanent bench, a caution line can be painted in the area of operation only.

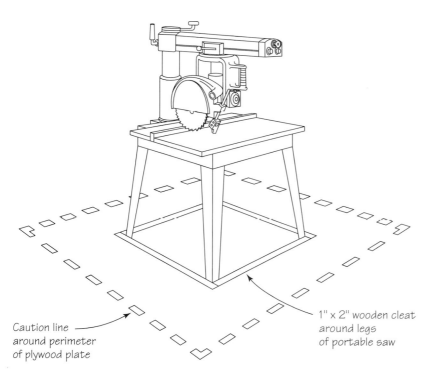

Caution line around perimeter of plywood plate

1" x 2" wooden cleat around legs of portable saw

For a portable radial saw it is best to make a "stabilization plate" with a caution line drawn around the perimeter. Note the 1" × 2" cleats that hold the saw base in place.

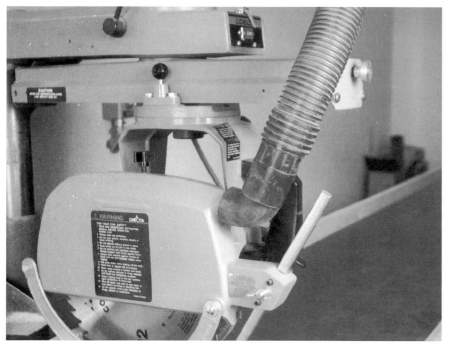

The sawdust exhaust port is part of the saw guard. A flexible tube is mounted to this port and connected to a vacuum, which can be located elsewhere in the shop.

be painted in the area of operation (see bottom figure page 29). If a stabilization plate is used for temporary installation, a line can be painted completely around the perimeter of the plate to indicate caution.

RADIAL ARM SAW DUST COLLECTION

As previously mentioned, the dust collection port is made as part of the guard. This makes it necessary to mount a vacuum tube from overhead. The vacuum tube must be flexible and allowed to travel along with the moving yoke that holds the blade (see figure bottom left). The vacuum itself can be mounted in a satellite position under the bench or elsewhere in the shop.

RADIAL ARM SAW ADJUSTMENT AND ALIGNMENT

The radial saw is comprised of many moving parts. The blade or cutter must be held securely on the arbor, which must be secured by the yoke and overarm. If any of these parts is out of adjustment, the accuracy of the cut will be in jeopardy. There are adjustment stops in the overarm, yoke and motor that are installed by the factory, normally at 0° and 45°, which will help gain a point of reference for all adjustments (see figures on page 31).

Adjustments

Although radial saws may differ from make to make, they will all have the same basic relationships and adjustments. Naturally, you should check your saw upon the initial setup and then periodically

There are adjustment stops in all three of the pivotal parts of the radial saw. If adjusted properly these make it easy to locate the most commonly used angles. The overarm rotation lock and stop are illustrated here.

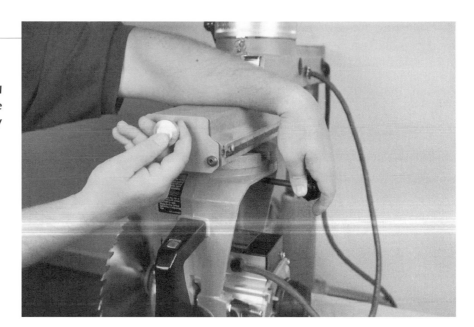

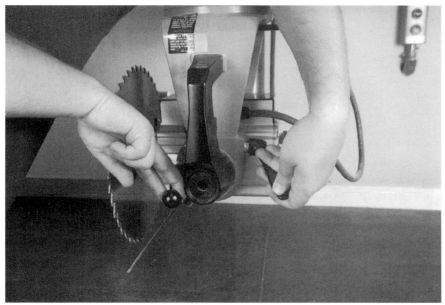

The motor swivel lock and stop.

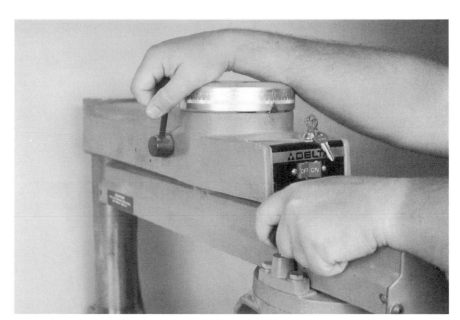

The yoke swivel lock and stop.

Adjustments

1. The overarm to the fence— The overarm is 90° to the fence during normal operation.
2. The blade to the table— The blade is 90° to the table during normal operation.
3. The pivotal yoke (which holds the motor) to the fence— The blade is parallel to the overarm during normal operation.
4. Depth of cut adjustment— The blade is ⅛" below the table surface during normal operation.

Before beginning the alignment process check that the saw table or bench is perfectly flat. If it is not flat, the use of shims would be in order.

according to your maintenance schedule. Every saw has a means by which to adjust the components built right into the tool. Read the owner's manual that is specific for your saw in order to make these adjustments.

ALIGNMENT

Every radial arm saw setup can be completed by using a combination of the four relationships just mentioned. Each time that I tune up my saw I assume that nothing is correct and start from the beginning. That way I am not "working backwards" in an effort to correct a problem that may have more than one cause.

Beginning with the table, I make sure that it is flat with the use of a simple straight edge or ruler (see figure top right). Sometimes the tops can warp or bend, depending on the rigidity of the underlying structure. The table should also be parallel to the overarm. With the blade set above the

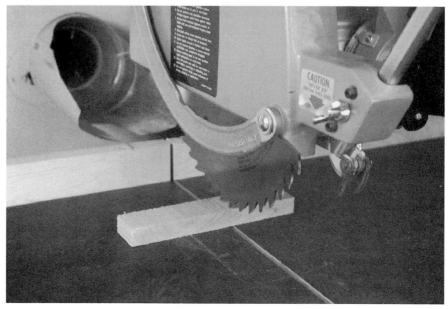

A dimensioned block of wood is used under the blade along the cut line as a "feeler gauge." In this way, the table can be verified as parallel to the blade.

table, I take a small block of wood and use it as a feeler gauge. With the blade raised above the table, I slip the block between the blade and table at different positions along the cut line (see bottom figure page 32). If the table is not parallel to the blade, it will need to be shimmed accordingly.

The backstop (or fence), which is part of the table, must be perfectly straight. I check this with a string across the entire length of the stop (see figure top right). If this stop is not straight and in line on both sides of the fence it will hold the material at an angle to the blade. As the length of the material being milled increases along the fence, this unplanned-for angle will also be increased.

A string is used to check that the fence is perfectly straight. An uneven fence can translate into inaccurate cuts.

RADIAL ARM SAW PARTS
The Overarm

Once the table top and fence have been confirmed to be flat and straight, I move on to relationship number one, the overarm to the fence. During normal operation this pivotal overarm will be at 90° to the fence. Again, the factory has installed a stop or indexing pin at both 90° and 45°. With the overarm against the 90° stop and locked, I draw a line on a wide piece of wood with a square and then cut along one side of the line (see figure middle right)—if the blade does not follow the line, I know that an adjustment of the stop is necessary. Once the 90° cut has been adjusted properly, the 45° stop will automatically be correct. When all is said and done with this correction, check that the miter scale on top of the machine is set at 0° for normal operation (see figure bottom right).

A square line is drawn on a wide piece of material to be cut. If the saw does not follow this line with the overarm in the normal position, an adjustment will have to be made.

After the blade has been confirmed to be 90° to the fence, reset the overarm scale to 0°. All other overarm angles can then be set accurately.

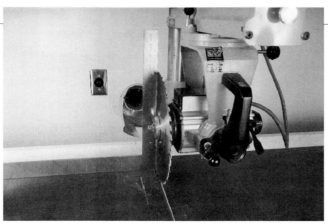

To adjust the blade perpendicular to the table, place a square between the teeth of the blade and the fence. Note that the square is as close to the center of the blade as possible.

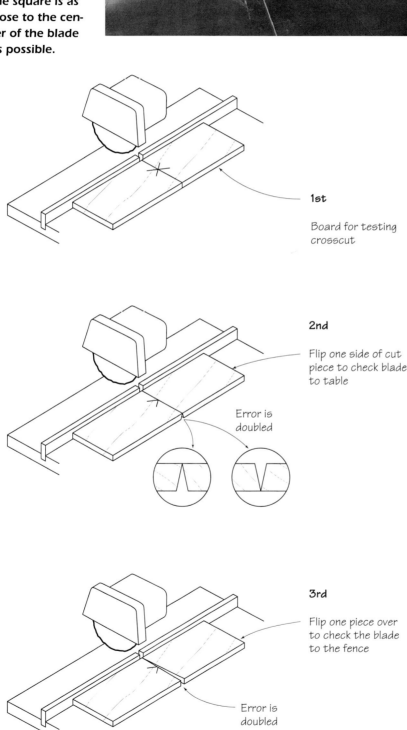

1st

Board for testing crosscut

2nd

Flip one side of cut piece to check blade to table

Error is doubled

3rd

Flip one piece over to check the blade to the fence

Error is doubled

After saw is aligned, make this simple "cut test." Flip one side of the material over and reposition it against the fence, inaccurate cuts will be apparent.

There is one final note on relationship number one: If there is a major inaccuracy when cutting along the penciled edge with the overarm set at the 90° stop, the entire body of the machine may not be sitting on the bench properly. This may be especially true if you built the bench or table for your saw. If this is the case, it will be necessary to adjust the whole machine or table one way or the other to make the major correction. (I would consider a major correction to be ¼″ or more on a 12″ cut.)

The Motor

The cut edge must be square to the stock placed against the table fence, and it must also be square to the table. Relationship number two, the blade to the table, will be the next matter of adjustment. I do this by placing a square against the table and the blade with the guard removed. The edge of the square should be placed between the teeth of the blade, which is slightly raised above the table. The square should also be as close as possible to the middle of the blade (see figure top left). It is important that the arm and carriage clamps are locked so that the blade is in a stationary position in front of the fence.

After this relationship has been adjusted, I make a test cut on a wide piece of scrap and make a simple test against the fence. Once cut, flip one of the two pieces over and rebutt against the fence—if there is any error it will be doubled and very noticeable to the eye (see figure bottom left). Once verified, I make sure that the angle indicator is set at 90° so that all other angles can be set reliably with ease.

The Yoke

The yoke to the fence is the third relationship on the list. In normal operation the blade is in direct line with the overarm. The motor, which holds the blade on an arbor, is connected to the yoke, which has the ability to pivot under the overarm. When turned 90°, or parallel to the fence, the saw can be used for ripping and shaping operations.

With the indexing pin set in the yoke for normal operation, I first check that the blade is not "heeling" in the cut. Heeling is an undesirable situation caused by the back teeth of the blade not cutting in the same line as the front teeth; in essence, the heel will make a second cut that causes fraying, burning or binding, depending on the degree that it is out of alignment. I check for this problem by crosscutting a wide piece of 1½"

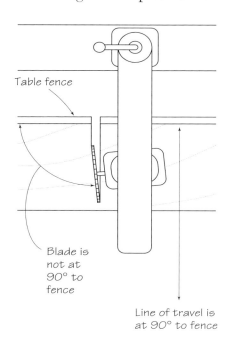

Table fence

Blade is not at 90° to fence

Line of travel is at 90° to fence

Guard not shown to demonstrate heeling

"Heeling" is an undesirable situation caused by the back teeth not cutting on the same line as the front teeth.

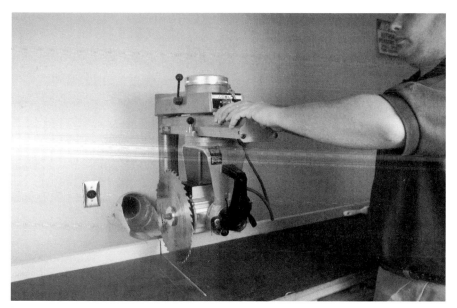

The column should be held snugly in the base. Hold one hand at the base while pushing up on the overarm. There should not be any play.

stock. After the front teeth have completed the cut, I check both edges for pronounced radial marks on the back. If this is the case, it is a simple matter of adjusting the yoke to the right or left, accordingly.

Depth of Cut Setting

For relationship number four, depth of cut adjustment, it is important to have an understanding of the column. A cylindrical member that connects the overarm to the saw base, the column moves up or down via a handle, normally at the top of the tool. There should not be any play within the column where it is attached to the base or overarm. I hold one hand where the column meets the split base at the bottom and push up slightly on the overarm (see figure above); any movement at all indicates that the base should be tightened.

If the column is hard to move up and down, it is either too tight at the base or in need of lubrication. There is a fine line to this adjustment: The column should not

be loose within the base, but should move freely enough to adjust easily. When adjusting the column, I like to move it the full distance of travel in both directions to make sure that it is properly lubricated and tight enough to not have play. After doing this I reset the blade ⅛" below the table surface for normal operation. This is done initially with the saw running and the blade being lowered slowly into the table. Once lowered, it is pulled across the table.

The Roller Bearings

The roller bearings within the overarm are adjustable (see top figure page 36). I make sure that these bearings are clean and well oiled before trying to adjust them. There are normally four rollers, two of which are adjustable on one side. If the yoke assembly pulls too tight, the two adjustable eccentric bearings will have to be backed off. If there is any play where the bearings meet the track they will have to be tightened.

The Blades

All of my thoughts regarding the maintenance of blades for the table saw will also apply to the radial saw. Dull blades can cause the same inaccuracy as misalignment of the tool. Even when the blade is sharp I am always careful not to pull it across the work faster than it will cut. This can cause the motor to slow, which will result in a rough cut or burning on the edges.

If the arbor is the same diameter as the arbor on your table saw, you may be able to interchange blades. Never put a larger blade than is recommended by the factory on either tool, but there is no problem with a smaller blade. I can use a 10″ dado set for both my 10″ table saw and my 12″ radial saw because the arbors are the same size.

The Arbor

On the radial saw, the arbor is part of the motor. It is in essence a direct-drive machine. To check that the arbor bearings are not bad, I hold the blade gently on each side and make sure that there is no play. If there is play in the arbor then it is the motor bearings that are bad. This will also be evident if you notice a wobble or hear a clicking noise when the machine is turned off and coming to a stop.

The arbor assembly is comprised of a threaded shaft with a fixed flange, a washer and a nut. I check the fixed flange with a dial indicator for possible runout; there should not be more than 0.004″ of runout at the flange. If a dial indicator is not available and you suspect a problem, check the blade to see if it is warped, and make sure that it is sitting flat against the arbor flange. The flange and arbor

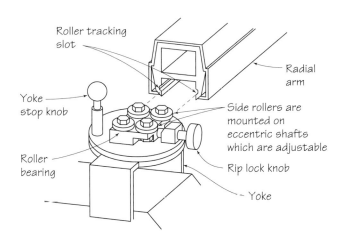

Roller tracking slot

Yoke stop knob

Roller bearing

Radial arm

Side rollers are mounted on eccentric shafts which are adjustable

Rip lock knob

Yoke

The roller bearings should be adjusted within the overarm. There is a fine line of adjustment that will allow the bearings to move freely within the carriage.

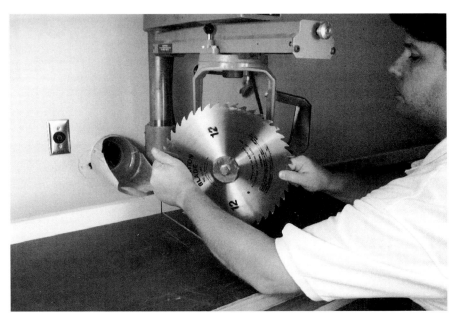

To check the arbor bearings, hold the blade with both hands and gently apply pressure from side to side. There should not be any play in the arbor.

washer should be flat and free of dirt and burrs.

CLEANING, OILING AND WAXING

The roller bearings column and all pivotal parts require constant cleaning. Lacquer thinner on a cotton rag works well to wipe these parts down. After cleaning, I like to apply a light machine oil to these parts. I am careful not to get the oil on any of the clamp downs for the moving parts. Oil on the clamp downs makes it necessary to overt-

ighten, which will lead to premature wear and tear. Oil tends to attract dust, so a simple wipe down is in order to remove the excess after it has been applied.

I use the same carnuba wax on my table top and fence as described in chapter one. This is applied often, according to my maintenance schedule. Even though the work stays still on the table, it is necessary to slide the material on the bench. Waxing is also a good way to stay "in tune" with the bench and fence.

Radial Arm Saw
Troubleshooting at a Glance

1. Board is not square across the width

PROBLEM	SOLUTION
Overarm is not 90° to fence	Reset overarm; check 90° stop
Blade is "heeling"	Adjust the yoke so blade pulls parallel
Dull blade	Have the blade sharpened

2. Cut edge is not square

PROBLEM	SOLUTION
Blade is not 90° to the table	Reset motor and blade to 90°
Excessive material overhang:	Make sure that material is supported for entire length

3. Bevels are not accurate

PROBLEM	SOLUTION
Blade not set to proper angle	Check the angle indicator and autostops—make test cuts on scrap

4. Blade drags; kerf wider than normal

PROBLEM	SOLUTION
Blade is "heeling"	Adjust yoke so that blade pulls parallel
Dull blade	Have the blade sharpened

5. Work moves away from fence

PROBLEM	SOLUTION
Fence is not perfectly straight	Check the fence with a string line

6. Kickback, or blade does not pull easily

PROBLEM	SOLUTION
Roller bearings in overarm too tight or too loose	Adjust and oil roller bearings
Dull blade	Have blade sharpened

7. Excessive sawdust during cut

PROBLEM	SOLUTION
Exhaust port in guard clogged	Remove blockage
Vacuum full or not hooked up	Check vacuum

8. Dado depth is not uniform

PROBLEM	SOLUTION
Table is not parallel to blade	Shim the table parallel

9. Blade binds

PROBLEM	SOLUTION
Excessive overhang of material	Make sure that material is supported for entire length

10. Excessive splintering at bottom of cut

PROBLEM	SOLUTION
Cap in table top is wider than the blade	Replace the top or make an insert piece in the top under the blade

Radial Arm Saw

ALL OPERATIONS:

✔ Blade tightened on arbor
✔ Guard set and locked
✔ All pivotal parts locked
✔ Fence straight and table top flat
✔ Table top and fence waxed
✔ No obstructions around saw
✔ Safety glasses on

CROSSCUTTING OPERATIONS:

✔ Material securely against fence
✔ Material fully supported on table
✔ Blade in line with overarm
✔ Blade 90° to table
✔ Overarm set and blade set at proper angle

RIPPING OPERATIONS:

✔ Blade set in proper direction
✔ Blade set parallel to fence
✔ Yoke thumbscrew tightened on overarm

CHAPTER THREE

The Band Saw

In my mind, a wood shop is just not complete without a band saw. Both the home shop enthusiast and the cabinetmaker in business quickly learn to appreciate the usefulness of this tool when it comes to cutting curves. This saw is also used in the field by many professionals such as finish carpenters and floor installers where a multitude of radius cuts are required. For those who lack the knowledge or are unwilling to learn, this piece of equipment does have a reputation for being hard to adjust. The fact is that, with a little know-how and patience, it is one of the easiest power tools to keep maintained.

The band saw derives its name from the type of blade it uses. A narrow strip of steel that is available in many widths and tooth configurations, this blade is formed into a continuous "band." Unlike the circular-type blades, the band saw blade is thin and cuts with very little waste. Depending on the width of the blade that is used, this tool is ap-

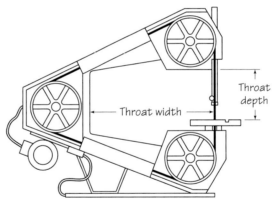

Three wheel type

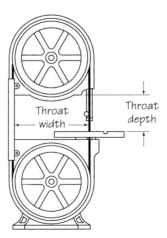

Two wheel type

There are both two- and three-wheel vertical band saws. Note: The three-wheel type usually has a much deeper throat, which allows a greater horizontal depth of cut.

The guide post and guard should be set at ¼″ above the work. This is for safety reasons, and to ensure that the blade does not flex during the cut.

propriate for either radius cutting or straight-cut operations such as the re-sawing of wide boards.

TYPES OF BAND SAWS

I categorize the band saw into two types. The two-wheel type takes up less floor space in the shop and requires a shorter, less expensive blade. The three-wheel type is a little larger, but offers a deeper throat width, which equates into a little more versatility. This latter type requires a little more maintenance and is more difficult to keep tracking properly. The depth of cut, which is not necessarily affected by the number of wheels in the saw, is also a very important concern. Maximum blade width and motor size are determined by the diameter of the wheels and the actual size of the saw. The re-sawing of thick lumber would re-

quire a 1″-wide blade and a ¾-horsepower motor as a minimum.

Most band saws offer a tilting table that is slotted to accept a sliding miter gauge. The table usually has a fence attachment, which is sometimes optional, to allow for the many types of ripping operations that are possible. Another option offered by some manufacturers is a depth-of-cut extender that will raise the body of the saw and require a longer blade. The most important thing to look for when buying any size band saw is well balanced wheels that have good bearings. To ensure against future headaches, be cautious of the cheaper saw that looks "as good" as one that costs twice as much.

BAND SAW SAFETY

As always, I feel compelled to devote some time to safety as it ap-

plies to the use of each tool. In the safety sections of the previous chapters I have already written about the safety concerns of power tools in general. If this is the only tool that you intend to operate, I recommend that you go back and review at least those safety segments of each chapter.

The well adjusted and maintained band saw with a sharp blade is the best beginning to safe operation. A clutterfree work space with good lighting, especially in the area of operation, is only common sense. The blades do break—at the weld after many hours of use, and as a result of tension, dullness, knots in the wood, etc.—so with this tool I make it a habit not to stand to the side of the blade at any time. Unlike the circular-type saws, if a blade breaks, the tendency is for it to unwind from the

Safety Rules

- Do not attempt to feed the work faster than the blade will cut.
- Choose the right blade for the job.
- Make sure that the table tilt knob and guide post are clamped down before beginning any operation.
- Keep the work firmly down on the table, and against the fence or miter gauge when these accessories are used.
- Push the work straight past the teeth without exerting pressure toward either side.
- Always set the guard ¼" above the work before every new operation.
- Never stand to the side of the saw during operation.
- Always unplug the tool before making any adjustments.
- Never use a dull or overly fatigued blade.
- Always use eye protection.

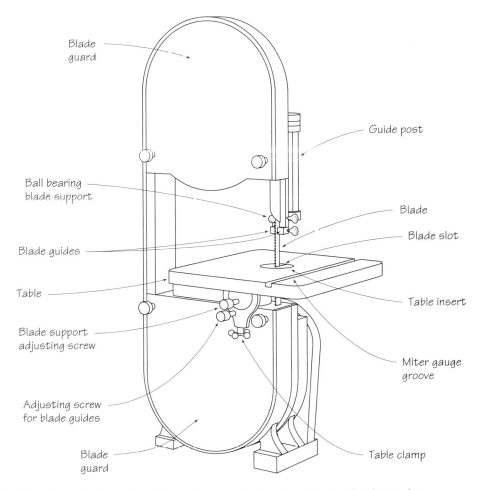

This is a typical (two-wheel) band saw anatomy. The three-wheel type has the same basic anatomy with the addition of the third wheel.

side. This does not always happen, but better safe than sorry.

There is a blade guard provided with every band saw on the market. These are adjusted each time the material thickness changes. The rule of thumb here is that this guard should be set at approximately ¼" above the material being cut (page 40)—this will allow enough room above the work to see and follow the line that you wish to cut on. Read and digest all of the information provided with

the saw to fully understand all of the specific safety concerns for that tool. If you buy a used saw that does not have a manual, I highly recommend that you take the time to write or call the manufacturer, who will be happy to send you one.

As with all of my tools, I keep an operational checklist, like the one printed at the end of this chapter, tacked up by my saw. A quick review of this list reminds me of the particular operational and safety concerns related to this saw.

Band Saw
Maintenance Schedule

Serial Number:

Date of Purchase:

Parts to be changed: Rubber belts (yearly), rubber tires around wheels (2 years), blades (6-8 hours)

Parts to be aligned (3 hours): Wheels, side guide blocks, thrust bearings, blade tension, guide post, table top

Parts to be oiled (5 hours):   Guide post, thrust bearings, wheel bearings

Parts to be waxed (1-2 hours): Table top, Fence, Miter slide

Date	Hours of Operation	Maintenance Notes

A separate maintenance schedule should be kept for each machine in the shop. Note that all pertinent information is listed along with a section for notes on adjustment.

BAND SAW ASSEMBLY AND INSTALLATION

As with all stationary power tools, this saw must be properly assembled and installed before operation. Even if the saw has been assembled at the factory, do not take for granted that all is correct. Before the saw is plugged in, check it closely against the schematic—while doing this you will become familiar with the tool's anatomy. Conceptually, all band saws have a similar format regardless of size or the number of wheels they use (see figure page 41). Re-oil all moving parts during the initial parts check or assembly process.

BAND SAW MAINTENANCE

I always make myself a maintenance schedule specific for each tool as soon as it enters my shop. As seen in the chart on page 42, the schedule for the band saw would include the date of purchase, serial number, and all parts that should be oiled, greased or changed. I also make note of when I change the blade; this way I have some idea how many hours each blade has been used, and can throw them away before they break. If your saw is belt driven, the belt should be changed once a year. The better band saws have rubber around the wheels, which helps the blade track properly. These should also be changed once a year or more often, depending on the usage. After the initial set-up, and each time the saw is adjusted, I make notes and enter the date for everything that is done.

BAND SAW LOCATION

There are two basic categories of band saw. The bench type is de-

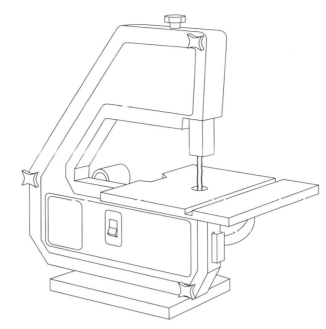

According to the space available in the shop and the scope of the work, a bench model band saw may be adequate for your needs.

Bench model

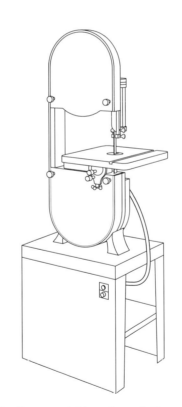

The floor model band saw is the most common type found in cabinet and furniture shops. These saws are much more versatile than the bench model due to the larger wheels and additional horsepower.

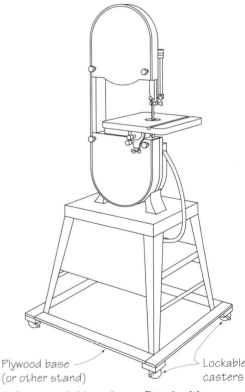

Plywood base (or other stand)

Lockable casters

A floor model band saw fitted with lockable casters can roll around within the shop for greater efficiency and versatility.

signed to mount to a bench and does not take up any floor space per se. This type is not really suited for re-sawing operations, but do be careful not to mount it in a way that limits the length of cut. The ideal way to mount this saw is on a lockable lazy Susan, or to simply clamp it to the bench so that it can be adjusted. The second type is the floor model that has its own base or stand. This type should have a specific place in the shop, but should not necessarily be bolted to the floor. I have lockable casters mounted to the base of my saw that enable me to pivot the saw around within its space when re-sawing long boards, etc.

The band saw is an important tool, but is not part of the "golden triangle" of operation. If it is a floor model, in the ideal shop situation this tool should be placed against a wall with plenty of room all around (see figure at right). The wall should be one that is away from the table saw, radial arm saw and jointer. A caution line should be drawn on the floor all around it, since the area of operation includes front, side and back.

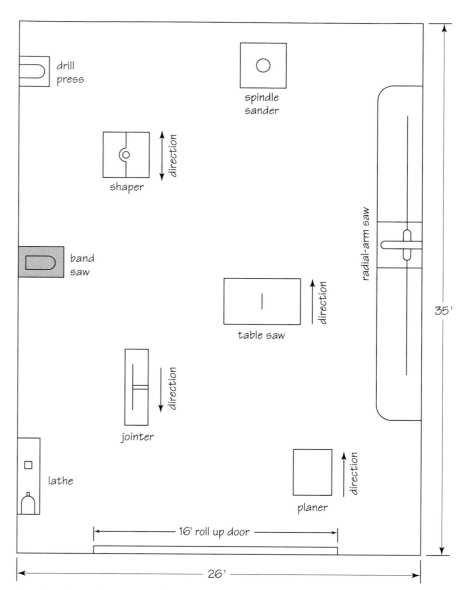

The band saw is not considered part of the "golden triangle." It should be placed perpendicular to a wall, with as much cutting distance as possible on each side of the blade.

BAND SAW DUST COLLECTION

The band saw is basically an enclosed tool. By nature of the design, the blade is sandwiched between a fixed and a removable housing. The fixed housing has a port at the bottom for the removal of sawdust. It is extremely important that the waste be exhausted at all times during operation; if not exhausted, material will build up quickly and cause a multitude of

problems. The most obvious problem would be sawdust and wood chips collecting between the wheel and blade causing the premature wearing of parts, including the blade.

I use a simple shop vacuum that is wired directly into the saw. When the machine is turned on, the vacuum is engaged automatically. By making the vacuum part

of the tool, it is impossible for me to forget to turn it on. A central dust collection system is nice (if one can be afforded), but I like to reserve the capacity for the bigger tools that are used more often. If a central system is used, be sure to place a switch close by the band saw, and include the system on your checklist so its use is a matter of routine.

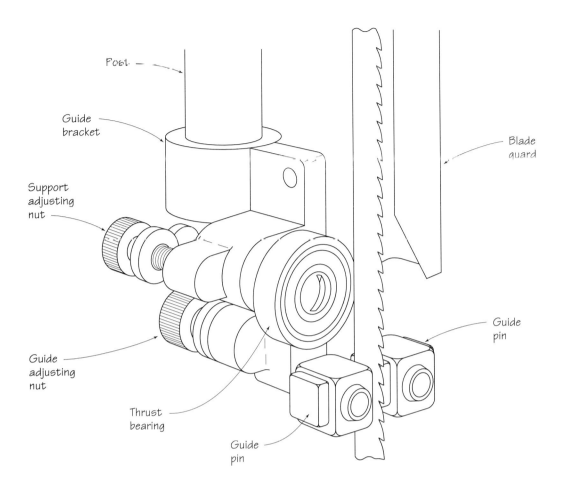

Post

Guide bracket

Support adjusting nut

Guide adjusting nut

Thrust bearing

Guide pin

Blade guard

Guide pin

There are two sets of guide components one above and one below the table. The upper set of components is mounted to the guide post, which is adjustable.

BAND SAW ADJUSTMENT AND ALIGNMENT

Although the band saw is less complex than the table or radial arm saws, it requires as much care and maintenance to keep it running trouble free. The blade must track properly on the wheels with the correct tension according to size. If the wheels are out of line or worn, the blade will tend to wander. There are two sets of guide components one above and one below the table (see figure above). They are made up of side guide blocks to keep the blade from twisting, and thrust bearings that keep the blade from being pushed off the wheels. Both the side blocks and thrust bearings must be set properly for each blade width.

Band Saw Adjustments

Band saws are available in many shapes, sizes and configurations. There are both vertical and horizontal models made for different aspects of woodworking. The most common types used in woodworking shops are the 12″ and 14″ vertical floor models. After making the initial inspection of your particular machine, read your owner's manual thoroughly and learn how to make these adjustments.

Adjustments

1. Wheel angle—The top wheel is adjustable for pitch, which will govern the tracking of the blade.
2. Blade tension—The top wheel can be raised and lowered to install blades.
3. Guide components—The guide blocks and thrust bearings can be adjusted to suit the blade size.
4. Guide post—There should be ¼″ of clearance between the material being cut and the bottom of the guide post assembly.
5. Table angle—The table is 90° to the blade during normal operation.

Band Saw Alignment

All band saw blade changes and setups will be completed with a combination of the five relationships just mentioned. Assume nothing when tuning your saw: It is best to start at the beginning each time a blade is changed. As with all machines, alignment is a matter of formula, which in time will become routine. Remember that it is a pleasure to operate a well aligned band saw that has a sharp blade.

BAND SAW PARTS
Installing the Blade

The first step in installing a blade is to remove the one that is presently on the machine. Unplug the tool, and remove the screw or rail that is used to align the table halves (see figure top right). With the saw cover off, unscrew or raise the blade guard and remove the throat plate (see figure bottom right). Release the blade tension by lowering the top wheel via the tension knob, which is normally located at the top of the saw.

Using both hands, slide the blade off the wheels and through the slot in the table. At this point I like to fold the old blade into thirds—even if it is going to be discarded. A very simple way to do this is to place one foot lightly on the inside bottom of the blade and then twist the top of the blade twice.

Once the blade has been removed, loosen the thrust bearings and side guides both above and below the table. The side guide assembly will have two adjustments: one that loosens the blocks that keep the blade from twisting, and another that allows the whole guide block assembly to move

The first step in changing a blade is to remove the screw or rail that is used to align the two table halves.

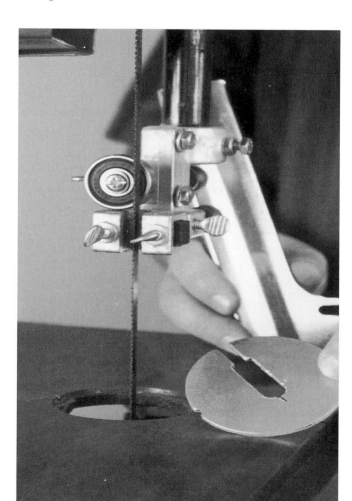

Before a blade can be dealt with, the saw cover must be opened and the throat plate removed.

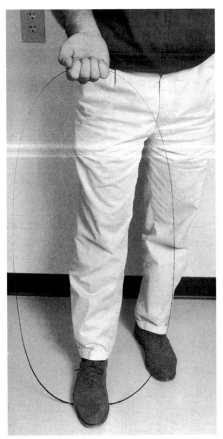

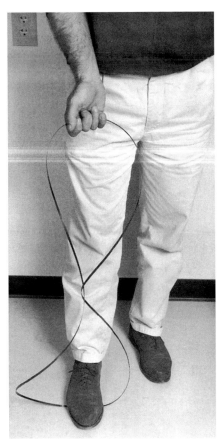

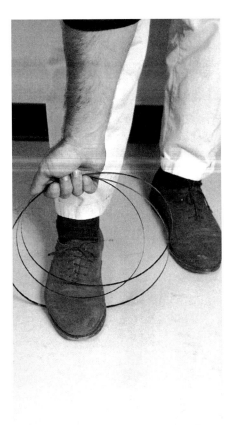

The blade should be folded into three loops before being stored. First, put one foot lightly on the bottom while twisting from the top down.

Twist the blade 360° moving toward your feet. The blade will be unfolded in a reverse manner when ready for use.

Continue toward your feet making three even loops.

backward or forward. This second adjustment allows the side blocks to be adjusted so that they are located behind the teeth of any given size blade (see top figure page 48).

Carefully unwind the blade to be installed in the reverse manner of how it was folded. Once unfolded, check to see that the teeth are pointed down—if not, grasp the blade with both hands and with your thumbs twist it around until the teeth are correct. With the teeth toward you, slide the blade through the slot in the table and over the wheels. At this point I apply enough pressure with the tension knob to take any slack out of the blade; that way the teeth will not rub on anything when I rotate the wheel by hand for the final tension adjustment. Most band saws have a built-in tension scale that indicates the proper pressure for each size blade.

If you have purchased a used saw, or if yours is older, you should check—and if need be replace—the tension spring so that the indicator will be accurate. One last special note: Always verify that the blades are the right length per the saw manufacturer's specifications. If they are not the correct size the tension indicator will not give an accurate reading, which, among other things, could cause the blade to break.

Before final tension is applied, make sure that the wheels of the saw are in line. This can be done by holding a straight edge against the wheels (see bottom figure page 48). If the wheels are not in line they must be adjusted before the blade will track properly. All saws are different in terms of the way this adjustment will be done. It may be a matter of changing the position of the bottom wheel or adding shims to the top wheel; check your owner's manual for the specific way your saw's wheels should be aligned. Fortunately this should only have to be done one time, if at all.

Tracking

With the blade tensioned properly per the tension gauge on the saw, it is now time to adjust the tracking. The blade should track in the center of the wheels. This is accomplished by tilting the top wheel one way or the other via the tilt knob, or screw, which is part of the saw. While rotating the wheels by hand with the guide components still backed off, slowly tilt the wheel until the blade stays in the middle (see top figure page 49). Lock the tilt knob and rotate the wheels more briskly by hand a few more times. Once satisfied that the blade is tracking properly, replace the cover, plug the machine back in, and turn it on momentarily. Watch to see that the blade does not jump forward or backward when the machine is turned on. If it does, the blade may not be tensioned properly, or the top wheel tilt will have to be adjusted again.

Once the blade is tensioned and tracked properly, and before the guide components are adjusted, the blade should be squared to the table. This is done by holding a small square behind the teeth of the blade and against the table (see bottom figure page 49). Once square, tighten the table tilt knob and set the 90° stop, which is usually under the back of the table.

Adjusting the Guide Components

As previously mentioned, the guide components prevent the blade from twisting and being pushed off the wheel during the cut. The guide assemblies both above and below the table must be adjusted to the width and thickness

Be sure that the side blocks, which hold the blade straight, are positioned behind the gullet of the teeth. The blade will push back and touch the thrust bearings during the cut.

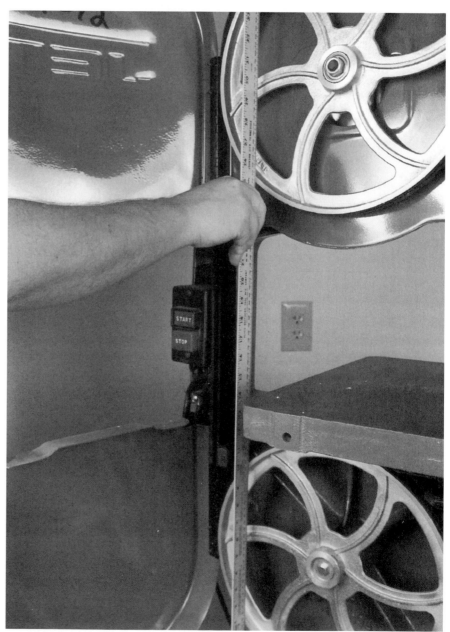

The wheels must be in line for the blade to track properly. Check this with a straight edge before installing the blade.

of the blade being used. The top guide assembly is mounted to the guide post, which in itself is adjusted up or down according to the thickness of material being cut. Lock the guide post, or upper assembly, in the middle position between the table and the top of its throw before beginning the adjustments (top page 50).

The thrust bearings, which are behind the blade, should be in line. Move the weld well below the table and past the bottom guides so that it does not interfere with the straight back of the blade (bottom page 50). I slip a piece of 220-grit sandpaper between the bearings and the back of the blade to achieve the proper setback (bottom page 51). After both bearings are tightened, check that they move freely and easily by spinning them with your finger. This is important because the blade will touch them during the cut, and any heat or friction generated by bad bearings might cause the blade to break.

The guide blocks located on each side of the blade are held by a guide holder, which is adjustable. I adjust the blocks by wrapping a piece of 400-grit sandpaper around the blade and pinching them together with my fingers (bottom page 51). Be sure that the block assembly is about $\frac{1}{32}''$ behind the gullet of the teeth because the blade does push back to the thrust bearings during the cut. Once adjusted, make sure everything is tightened. One special note: I always check the top guides and thrust bearing by eye for these tolerances each time the guide post is adjusted.

The blade should track in the center of the wheel. After the blade has been tensioned, this will be adjusted by tilting the top wheel.

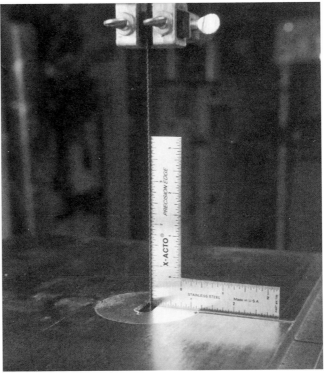

After the blade has been tracked, the blade can be squared to the table. With the guide post up, hold the square behind the teeth and adjust the table to 90°.

The Motor

A band saw can be either direct drive or belt driven. On a vertical saw it is the bottom wheel that is driven directly or via a pulley. On the belt-driven models it is important to make sure that the pulleys are in line at all times.

Misaligned pulleys can cause belts to break or motor bearings to go bad prematurely. As with any motor, you can tell that the bearings are bad by the annoying clicking sound the motor makes. If this is the case, it will be necessary to replace the motor or have it professionally reconditioned. A band saw motor with bad bearings will ultimately manifest itself through vibration that will cause alignment problems, broken blades, etc.

The Blades

The versatility of the band saw is apparent by the many different types of blades that are available. There are blades for cutting tight curves, ripping, and re-sawing boards on edge. According to the amount and set of the teeth the blade has, it will cut either fast and rough or slow and smooth. Tooth form, the pitch of the blade and the tooth set all determine how the blade will cut. The width of the blade determines if it should be used for a straight or curved cut. The smaller the width, the tighter the radius that can be made. All blades will leave some degree of edge marks; this is called "washboarding." The lines are straight (not circular) and can be minimized by a blade with less set on the teeth.

Maintenance-wise, it is false economy to have a dull blade sharpened. The cost of a new blade

Before adjusting the top guide components, lock the guide post half the distance of its throw (the middle position).

Before adjusting the thrust bearings, locate the weld in the blade and position it well below the table. The back of the blade acts as a straight edge for setting the bearings.

is less than the cost of sharpening. If the weld breaks on a new blade, it is worth having rewelded, but it should be done professionally.

The best way to stretch your blade dollars is by good alignment and adjustment of the machine. Another common sense tip would be to store the blades rolled and out of harm's way. I even store my old, dull blades that haven't broken for use when cutting scrap into firewood.

CLEANING, OILING AND WAXING

The guide post, roller bearings and all pivotal parts require frequent cleaning and oiling. As with the other machines, lacquer thinner on a clean cotton rag works best for cleaning. After cleaning, a light machine oil should be applied to keep the moving parts lubricated. Wipe off any excess oil, which will attract dust and defeat the purpose of the lubrication.

Even though the saw is connected to an exhaust system or vacuum, it is a good idea to remove the cover once in a while and blow the inside out. If a compressor is not available, use a vacuum cleaner to collect any excess dust from the wheels and bottom guide components. Dust tends to build up in the enclosed case and cause premature wear between the blade and wheels, as well as to the guides.

Wax should be applied to the table top and fence (if one is used). This would be applied often according to the maintenance schedule, and when an unusual amount of cutting is going to be done. A well waxed table will make the material glide better and will help reduce the amount of washboarding on the cut edges.

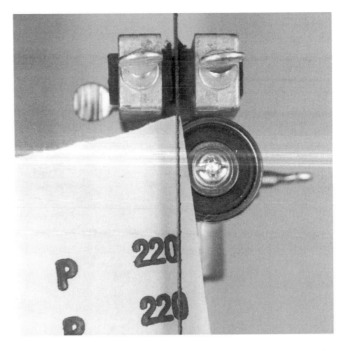

A piece of 220-grit sandpaper can be used as a gauge for setting the distance between the blade and the roller bearings.

A piece of 400-grit sandpaper can be wrapped around the blade as a guide for setting the guide blocks. Squeeze the blocks together against the paper without bending the blade.

Band Saw
Troubleshooting at a Glance

1. Excessive blade breakage

PROBLEM	SOLUTION
Blade tension is too tight	Use the tension guide (check blade length); check the tension spring
Saw clogged inside, not exhausting properly	Clean saw out each time you change a blade; make sure saw is exhausting properly
Blade too wide for radius being cut	Select proper width blade with the right tooth configuration (user's guide or blade manufacturer's guidelines)

2. Blade wanders from line being cut

PROBLEM	SOLUTION
Guide components not adjusted properly	Adjust side guide blocks and thrust bearings per adjustment section this chapter
Dull blade	Replace the blade
Wrong blade tooth or width configuration	Select proper blade

3. Cut is not square to surface

PROBLEM	SOLUTION
Table not set 90° to blade	With the guide up, check the blade to the table

4. Blade scrapes or makes clicking sound

PROBLEM	SOLUTION
Blade not tracking properly	Align tracking to center of the wheel and adjust roller bearings and guide blocks
Kinked or bent blade	Straighten or replace the blade

5. Cut surface is bowed

PROBLEM	SOLUTION
Blade is dull	Check tooth set and rake
Incorrect blade tension	Adjust tension (tighten) per the tension scale

6. Blade binds

PROBLEM	SOLUTION
Side guide blocks too tight	Loosen and adjust the side blocks

7. Blade does not stay on track

PROBLEM	SOLUTION
Top wheel angle is incorrect	Check that wheels are in line; set blade tension and wheel angle
Back roller bearings are set too far back	Adjust roller bearings to $\frac{1}{32}''$ behind the back of the blade

8. Roller bearings moving when saw is running free

PROBLEM	SOLUTION
Wheel tilt is set incorrectly	Adjust wheel tilt back and lock tilt
Thrust bearings are set too far forward	Reset thrust bearings and tighten them down

Band Saw

All Operations:

✔ Blade tension and tracking correct
✔ Guide blocks and thrust bearings set correctly
✔ Table top set and locked
✔ Guide post and guard set ¼″ above the work
✔ Table top (and fence) waxed
✔ No obstructions around the saw
✔ Safety glasses on

RE-SAW OPERATIONS:

✔ Sharp, wide blade installed
✔ Fence 90° to the table and locked

CROSS-CUT AND ANGLE OPERATIONS:

✔ Miter slide set and locked
✔ Table angle set and locked

CHAPTER FOUR

The Jointer

The jointer, or joint planer, is considered to be the most elite member of the "golden triangle" for woodworkers. This piece of equipment makes short work, minus the human error factor, of what used to be a laborious process with the hand plane. A key to proper stock preparation, the experienced woodworker realizes that this tool is by no means limited to edge-planing and surfacing. Other applications include wide rabbeting, chamfering, beveling, tenoning, tapering and decorative-leg shaping.

JOINTER ANATOMY

Consisting of two adjustable tables with a high-speed cutterhead between them, the jointer is a simple machine. The fence, which governs the amount of cutter that is exposed, slides across both tables and the cutter. The fence can also be adjusted at an angle to the bed for angle jointing and chamfering. This whole arrangement is

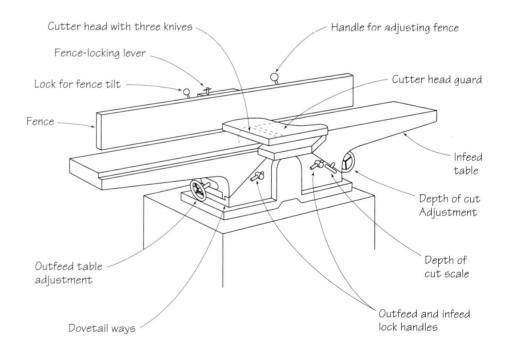

Cutter head with three knives

Fence-locking lever

Lock for fence tilt

Fence

Handle for adjusting fence

Cutter head guard

Infeed table

Depth of cut Adjustment

Depth of cut scale

Outfeed table adjustment

Dovetail ways

Outfeed and infeed lock handles

Regardless of the manufacturer, this would be a typical configuration for any jointer.

mounted to a base that houses the motor. The length of the knives mounted in the cutterhead determines the size of the jointer and the widest cut possible.

TYPES OF JOINTERS

Both beds are adjustable on the better jointers. The difference between those and the type with a fixed outfeed table is simple, but important. With the fixed outfeed table, it is necessary to remove the knives each time for sharpening and then to adjust them exactly to the back bed when reinstalled. Obviously this type is less expensive, but in the long run, there is no way of correcting any warp problems, short of grinding the bed. The fixed type is also limited in terms of potential. The fully adjustable jointer allows for tapered, concave, and many other types of design cuts.

Other variables to consider are the number of knives the cutterhead holds and the length of the bed. Obviously the more knives the cleaner the cut (if they are set properly). Different manufacturers' models range from two knives to four. The length of the bed determines how long a board can be accurately jointed and still remain straight and true. A typical cabinet or furniture shop employs a three-knife, eight-inch jointer with a five-foot, fully adjustable bed. For home use, a six-inch model would be more than adequate.

JOINTER SAFETY

From setting the knives through operation, the jointer is a particularly dangerous tool. Naturally there are basic rules of safe ma-

The jointer fence governs both the width and the angle of cut. There are adjustments and lockdowns for both of these functions.

chinery operation. A clutterless environment free of distractions, and working with well oiled and maintained equipment are good for starters. Beyond that, we also have to be fully aware that this tool is not for beginners. Total respect and understanding are in order every time the switch is turned on.

The pivoting guard should be in place, and should be used for every operation (page 56). The knives, which are mounted in the cutterhead, are held in place by a wedge (or gib) and lock screws. These must be tightened down properly or the blades could come loose once the high-speed cutter revolves. I always make a second tightening pass once all of the

knives have been set to the proper height. Make sure that there is enough clearance between the knives and both beds, and on each side of the cutterhead, before the machine is turned on. Another thing to remember is that the knives reach a point after many sharpenings where they become too small to use. It is best to discard them if they are smaller than ½" high.

Read your owner's manual and all of the operational information that you can before using the jointer for the first time. A good rule to remember for this and any other power tool is that "They only bite once!"

The jointer's pivotal guard is extremely important in terms of safety, and should be used for every operation.

Safety Rules

- Do not cut deeper than the cutter will allow.
- Be sure that the stock is clean and free of grit.
- Always unplug the tool before changing or sharpening the blades.
- Never operate this tool without the guard.
- Always use a pushstick if the material is shorter than the fence.
- Never pass your hand above the cutterhead during operation.
- Always keep the work held securely against the fence and table.
- Never joint a round or concave piece or any piece smaller than ½″.

JOINTER ASSEMBLY AND INSTALLATION

Before the jointer can be operated for the first time it must be properly assembled and completely checked over. Ninety percent of the time this tool will come already assembled from the factory or distributor. In today's expanding tool market, some combination models are available. These table saw/jointer or jointer/surface planer models use the same motor to drive both tools. Often these models do require minimal assembly due to their size and the obvious shipping concerns. This will probably only be a matter of connecting the tool bodies to the drive and mounting them to the base.

Regardless of how the tool is received, it should be checked against the manufacturer's schematic. Sometimes there is a lock-down that is installed at the factory to keep the cutterhead from moving during shipping. Make sure that this is removed, and that the knives are tightened down properly. Check that both beds will move freely on their dovetail ways, and then lock them down once the tool has been adjusted properly. The fence system should move freely across the entire width of the cutterhead. The fence angle pivot adjustment should be checked, then locked down at 90° to the table for normal operation.

JOINTER MAINTENANCE

Once the machine has been checked, make yourself a maintenance schedule specific for the tool (page 57). This should include the date of purchase, serial number and any parts that must be oiled, greased or changed (belts).

The Jointer
Maintenance Schedule

Serial Number:

Date of Purchase:

Parts to be aligned (each time the knives are changed):   Infeed and outfeed tables, infeed depth indicator, fence to table, fence auto-stops, knives to outfeed table

Parts to be changed (1 year):   Rubber belts

Parts to be greased or oiled (5 hours):   Infeed and outfeed table dovetailed ways, fence mechanisms, guard pivot

Parts to be waxed (1-2 hours):   Table beds, Fence

Date	Hours of Operation	Maintenance Notes

A maintenance schedule should be designed and used for the jointer. This will list all of the parts to be changed, oiled, adjusted and maintained.

If yours is a combination type, the schedule would include both tools that are driven by the same motor.

With the jointer, I clean and lubricate the dovetail ways, fence travel and pivot after every five hours of use. If the jointer is belt driven (combination types are sometimes direct drive), I change the belt once a year regardless of usage. The knives will be either high-grade steel or carbide tipped. These should be changed or dressed when they become dull. If the knives are still sharp but have been nicked due to hard knots in the wood, they can be slightly offset from each other and then reset to height. Chipped knives will be apparent when the finished material has "roads," or raised areas, on the jointed surface. Be sure to note the date each time the tool has been cared for.

JOINTER LOCATION

A member of "the golden triangle," the jointer should be placed as close to the table saw operation area as possible. These two tools really do go hand in hand, so much so that the combination table saw/jointer was designed. In the ideal situation, the feed direction should be in the opposite direction of the table saw. This will save steps and make for a more efficient operation.

JOINTER DUST COLLECTION

The jointer does not produce dust per se. The chips or shavings are usually delivered, via a chute, onto the floor in front of the machine. For this reason, a specific vacuum system is an option. In the larger cabinet shops there is usually a

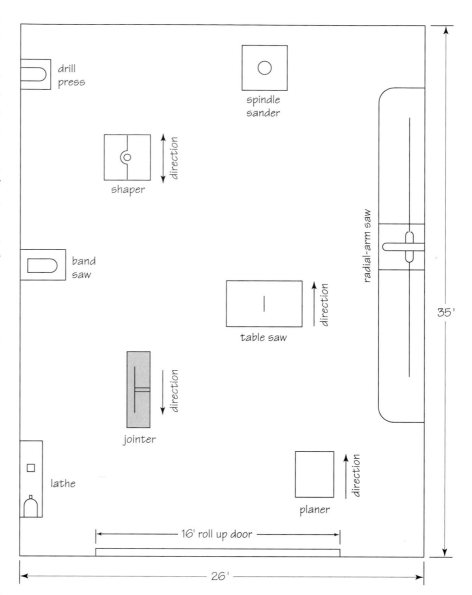

In the ideal situation, the jointer should be placed as close to the table saw as possible, and the feed should be in the opposite direction.

vacuum floor register near the jointer area into which the chips are swept. This is not necessary to the smaller concerns, but the waste should be picked up regularly so that it does not pile up and become dangerous to the operator. If the jointer that you employ is a part of a combination tool, there may be a central exhaust port. In this case it is important that both tools be exhausted by a vacuum or dust collector.

JOINTER ADJUSTMENT AND ALIGNMENT

The jointer is comprised of several moving parts that must be perfectly aligned and work in conjunction with each other. If any of these parts are misaligned, the machine will produce counterproductive cuts, which will only cause frustration. In short, the infeed and outfeed tables must be in line with each other, the knives should be level with the outfeed table at their apex, or highest point, and the fence should be at 90° to the table during normal operation. There are adjustment stops in the fence mechanism, usually at 90° and 45° (top right).

Jointers range in size from 4″ to 36″ of cutterhead, and come with beds of many different lengths. Regardless of size, they all have the same basic principles and relationships. Every jointer has the means to adjust the components built into its design. Check the owner's manual that is specific for your machine to learn how to make these adjustments.

The jointer fence is 90° to the bed during normal operation. Some jointer fences will have autostops at both 90° and 45°.

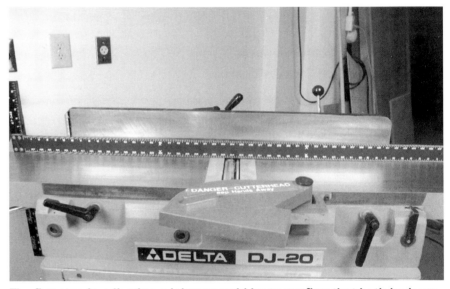

The first step in adjusting a jointer would be to confirm that both beds are in line with each other. The straight edge that is used should be as long as both of the beds combined.

Jointer Alignment

To begin with, as previously mentioned, the tables must be flat and on the same plane with each other. This should be checked with a straight edge that is at least as long as both beds combined (figure 4-7). Raise the infeed table so that it is on the same plane as the outfeed table. Rotate the cutterhead so that the knives will not interfere with the ruler. First check each table individually to make sure that there are no warps. The tables should then be checked as one, both lengthwise and diagonally, to make sure that they are flat. These are the primary things that should be looked at before purchasing any used jointer. The whole function of this tool depends on the tables being flat and true.

After making these checks, you may realize that either the tables are not properly aligned or that the tables are not parallel to each other. This second situation is correctable. If you find that the individual tables are warped in any manner there is a problem that can only be corrected by resurfacing the bed.

Jointers are designed so that

Adjustments

1. The depth of cut—This is governed by the infeed table, which can be adjusted up or down.
2. The width of cut—This is governed by the fence, which moves perpendicularly across the cutter area.
3. The angle of cut—This is governed by the fence pivoting mechanism.

they can be adjusted and aligned to compensate for the wear and tear of use. The dovetailed ways (top right) will have a series of screws through the sides or inside on each bed (unless the outfeed bed is fixed). Tightening these set screws will usually remedy the "sagging bed" syndrome. Once the screws have been tightened and the beds are in line, check that the bed will still move freely. If not, you may have to remove the bed from the tool body to clean and grease the ways. After the beds have been aligned, bring them to a level position with the straight edge so the depth scale can be set at the 0 position (bottom right). At this point I would like to mention that it is completely "uncool" to sit on, or ever set anything on, the beds of your jointer. Conversely, this tool should never be carried or moved around by the beds.

When the jointer tables and cutterhead with sharp knives are in perfect alignment, the work will pass smoothly across from one bed to the other (top page 61). The knives should be set even with the outfeed table when they are at the highest point of the cutting circle. If the outfeed table is too low, the work will be planed in an arch or drop at the end of the cut and create a "snipe" (middle page 61). If the outfeed table is too high, the work will snag on the back bed after it passes the knives, which will also create an arch in the work piece (bottom page 61).

Jointer Knife Adjustment

Regardless of the number of knives in the cutterhead, they should be changed or adjusted one at a time. This has to do with the

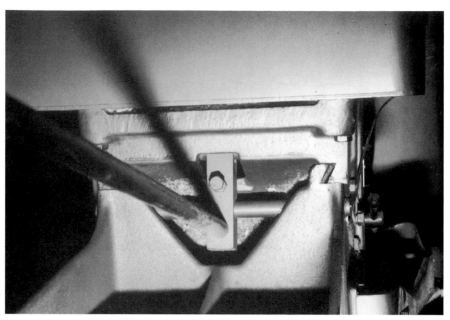

Jointer beds travel on a dovetailed way system. This helps ensure that the beds will not "rack," or loosen, due to the vibration of use.

The infeed table governs the depth of cut. All jointers have a calibrated scale that indicates the amount of material about to be removed. This scale should be set to 0 when both beds are on the same plane.

stress on the cutterhead, or lack of it, and is usually a recommendation of the manufacturer. The cutterhead is slotted to receive the knives; blade wedges or "gibs" hold the knives in place (top page 62). Each cutterhead system is a little different, so check your owner's manual to see how your knives would be removed.

It is a good idea to have more than one set of knives on hand. Just like circular saw blades, jointer knives should be sharpened professionally. It is very important that these be sharpened absolutely straight and with the correct bevel. So while one set is at the sharpener's, the other one is in the tool. This way you can change the blades one at a time as recommended above, and there is no downtime for the jointer. There are two schools of thought on resetting the knives. One suggests that the knives be aligned (or set to height) to the cutterhead; the other method uses the outfeed table as a point of reference. I favor the second method for a very simple reason: The cutterhead itself might be ever so slightly misaligned with the tables from left to right. By setting the knives to height with the back table, any misalignment of the cutterhead would be corrected.

One technique that I favor for adjusting the knives employs the use of a magnetic jig. There are a number of these on the market that are all very similar. Quite simply these hold the knives in place according to the outfeed table while the knife is being tightened in the cutterhead (bottom right). Some jointers have springs or screws under each knife that push

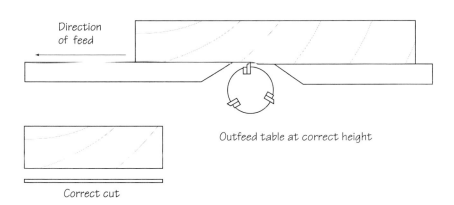

Outfeed table at correct height

Correct cut

When the jointer beds and cutters are properly aligned, the stock will pass smoothly from the infeed to the outfeed tables.

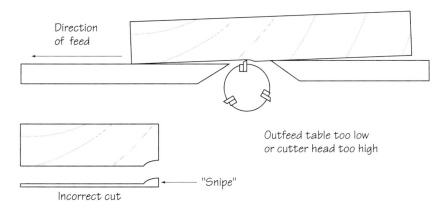

Outfeed table too low
or cutter head too high

"Snipe"

Incorrect cut

When the outfeed table is too low in relation to the knives, the stock will fall once it leaves the infeed table. This will cause a telltale "snipe" on the end of the stock.

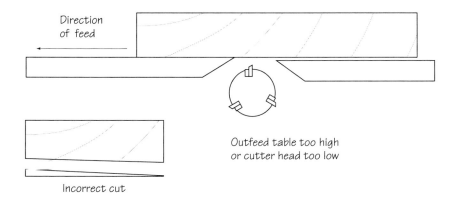

Outfeed table too high
or cutter head too low

Incorrect cut

When the outfeed table is too high in relation to the knives, the stock will snag or be stopped by the forward edge of the table.

them up to the magnetic bar while the gib is tightened. If this is not the case with your jointer, the magnet itself should hold the knife in place.

First, find the center of the cutterhead and knife with a straight edge, then scribe a line onto your fence (top page 63). This is the point at which the top of the knife should be even with the outfeed table and is at its highest point of the cutting circle. Some of the better jointers have a "pawl," or stop, built into them which locks the cutterhead into place at this position for each knife. Once this point has been located, you can set each knife edge with the magnetic bar and then tighten it down. Check that the knife also protrudes beyond the left edge of the back table about $1/16''$. This would be important for rabbeting operations, because it keeps the work from snagging on the back table edge. Be very careful while tightening the gib screws from the center outward. Just tighten them slightly until all of the screws are holding, and then make a second and final tightening pass. The knives will tend to ride up if you attempt to tighten them all the way the first time.

Once all of the knives have been set to the same height, remove the magnetic bar. Place the blade of a combination square on the outfeed table and slightly over the cutterhead and knives (bottom page 63). This straight edge should move $5/32''$ when rotating the cutterhead by hand. This should be checked at both ends of the cutter, and should be the same. If the square's blade does not move, and you have an adjustable outfeed table, move the

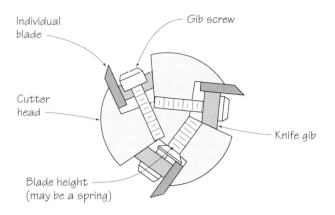

Individual blade · Cutter head · Gib screw · Knife gib · Blade height (may be a spring)

The typical cutterhead assembly will include: the cutterhead, the knives, the gibs and locking screws, and possibly two leveling screws or springs for each knife.

The magnetic jig is very helpful when setting the knives. There are many makes and models available in today's expanding tool market.

table slightly down. The thinking here is that once the knives' edges lose their keen (after the first few passes), the knives will be exactly level with the bed.

Adjusting the Jointer Fence

The fence is what supports the work at the desired angle while it passes across the cutters. The first step here is to make sure that the fence is straight and flat with a straight edge (top page 64). If it is not, there is a problem and the fence might have to be milled flat. Once the fence has been confirmed to be flat, set the fence in the 90° position with a square (middle page 64). This is the standard position for normal operation. If your fence has autostops for different positions, these will be automatically correct once the 90° position stop has been adjusted.

There are normally two mechanisms for locking the fence (bottom page 64). One is for locking the tilt and the other is for locking the travel, or width of cut position, into place. These may have a screw type of adjustment that governs the sensitivity of the lock. You never want these locks to be loose or they might decide to travel in the middle of a cut.

Adjusting the Guard

As previously mentioned, the guard is a very important part of the jointer, and the machine should never be operated without it. The guard operates on a pivot pin inserted directly into the infeed table. There is an adjustable spring that governs the tension of the guard. Ideally, there should be just enough tension to hold the guard firmly against the work

The knife will reach its highest point, or apex, at the center of the cutterhead. This point should be scribed into the fence for easy reference when setting the knives.

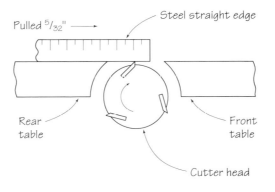

Pulled 5/32"

Steel straight edge

Rear table

Front table

Cutter head

When a new set of knives has been properly adjusted to the outfeed table, a one-foot rule will be pulled 5/32" when the cutterhead is rotated by hand.

The fence should be straight and true. This should be checked with a straight edge as part of the adjustment process.

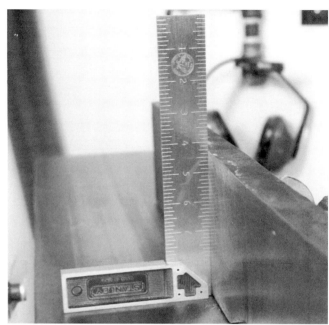

The jointer fence is set at 90° to the beds during normal operation. This should be checked on both the front and back tables.

Most jointers have a locking device each for the fence travel and the fence tilt. Both of these locks should be confirmed to be tight before the machine is operated.

piece, but not so much that the guard will "bang" against the fence once the cut has been completed.

CLEANING, OILING AND WAXING

If the cutterhead bearings are not sealed, and have a grease fitting, they will need to be maintained. Those and the dovetailed table ways should be greased with a lithium-type product at least once every six months, or as needed. This will help ensure longevity and keep these parts moving easily. The fence mechanisms should be cleaned and oiled after each five hours of use to keep them operating freely and easily. It is also a good idea to apply a little oil to the guard pivot so that it operates freely and always returns to the fence.

As with all our other equipment, the beds and fence should be waxed after one to two hours of operation. This ensures that the wood parts pass easily on all surfaces. Before the wax is applied to these surfaces it is always a good idea to clean them with lacquer thinner, which will remove any pitch buildup.

The Jointer
Troubleshooting at a Glance

1. Jointed edges are not square

PROBLEM	SOLUTION
The fence is not square to the tables, or fence tilt is not locked	Square the fence and make sure that it is locked
The tables are not on the same plane as the knives	Reset the knives per the knife section of this manual

2. Work drops and "snipes" after leaving infeed table

PROBLEM	SOLUTION
The outfeed table is set too low	Raise the outfeed table level with the knives

3. Work hits the edge of outfeed table

PROBLEM	SOLUTION
The outfeed table is too high	Bower the outfeed table level with the knives

4. Work planes in a curve

PROBLEM	SOLUTION
The outfeed table is not level with the knives	Set the outfeed table level with the knives
The knives are dull	Replace knives per this manual

5. Raised areas or "roads" in cut surface

PROBLEM	SOLUTION
The knives are chipped	Offset the knives slightly or replace them

6. Chattered or rippled surfaces

PROBLEM	SOLUTION
The knives are not all set to the same height	Reset the knives one by one per this manual

7. Cutter stalls

PROBLEM	SOLUTION
Belt does not have the proper tension or the pulley is loose	Check the pulleys and belt tension

The Jointer

ALL OPERATIONS:

✔ Infeed table set to correct depth
✔ Fence set to proper angle and locked
✔ Fence set to proper width and locked
✔ Guard is in place
✔ Both tables and fence are waxed
✔ No obstructions around the jointer
✔ Safety glasses are on

CHAPTER FIVE

The Shaper and Router

The shaper is one of the most important tools in any professional cabinet or furniture shop. Although it is not your everyday piece of equipment for the home craft shop, being aware of its existence can only help. Primarily used to produce shaped edges and mouldings, it excels like no other tool for all kinds of architectural woodwork. Grooving, fluting and face shaping are just a few of the operations that a shaper is capable of doing. Although many of these same operations are possible with the handheld router, the shaper is a stationary tool that has more power and larger cutters.

In recent years, competition within the home-use tool industry has made the shaper a more affordable tool. There are several good manufacturers that offer smaller, less expensive models that are very reliable. Even commercial cabinet shops employ the use of these smaller ½″ shapers for certain operations. Large or small, all shapers

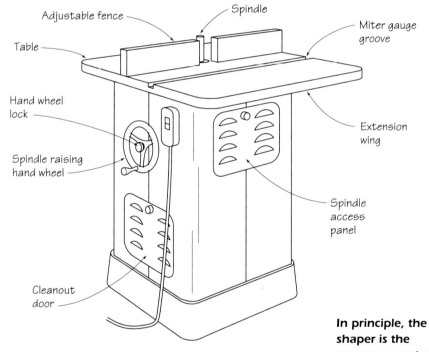

Adjustable fence — Spindle — Miter gauge groove — Table — Hand wheel lock — Spindle raising hand wheel — Cleanout door — Extension wing — Spindle access panel

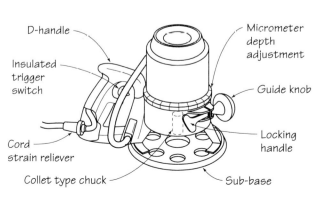

D-handle — Micrometer depth adjustment — Insulated trigger switch — Guide knob — Cord strain reliever — Locking handle — Collet type chuck — Sub-base

In principle, the shaper is the same as a router that has been inverted and mounted to a table. While these are both considered to be "spindle tools," the obvious differences would be size and power.

and routers operate on the same principles and require the same maintenance and adjustments.

TYPES OF SHAPERS AND ROUTERS

The shaper and the router are basically the same. They are motors with direct-drive shafts that can be fitted with cutters. The router can be hand held or mounted in a table. Routers come in many varieties, but in the wood shop we are concerned only with the fixed base and plunge base routers. The fixed base is the more common type of router. The depth of cut is adjusted by raising or lowering the motor inside of a housing. Another type of router is the plunge base type. The router base rides on adjustable springs. The depth of cut is fixed, but is not arrived at until pressure forces the base into the cut. This type of router is not recommended for installtion in a router table. We will concentrate on the fixed base type.

The shaper consists of a table mounted to a heavy base that has an adjustable spindle in the center. The spindle holds the cutters, which are usually of the three-wing type. In principle, the shaper is just a larger version of a router that has been inverted and mounted to a table. The spindle on the shaper, normally ½", ¾" or 1" in diameter, can be adjusted up or down to accommodate whatever setup is desired. There is an adjustable fence that is used for edge and face shaping. The table has been slotted to accept the miter gauge, and also has several appropriately placed

The shaper table has a miter gauge slot, which is also used when aligning the fence. A taper pin is inserted into one of the "threadless" holes close to the spindle when freehand or pattern shaping is done.

holes milled into it. A taper pin is inserted into one of these holes to serve as a starting point when freehand shaping operations are performed (above).

SHAPER AND ROUTER SAFETY

The shaper and router are considered to be some of the more dangerous tools because they operate at a high speeds (5,000-12,000 rpm). The cutters are hard to guard all the way around, and are 50 percent exposed when a fence is used. Use of the guards and holddowns provided with the tools whenever possible is highly recommended. Also, most shapers have a means of reversing direction located on the motor itself or as part of the power switch. This reversing capability allows the cutters to be turned over and the spindle to rotate in either direction. As with the router, the knives can only cut in one direction. Be sure and read a good operational handbook before using any shaper for the first time.

Shaper and Router
Maintenance Schedule

Serial Number (shaper):
　　　　　　　(router):

Date of Purchase:

Parts to be changed (1 year):　Shaper drive belt
　　　　　(when needed):　Router collet, and base plate

Parts to be aligned (each　　　Shape fence, cutter, and spindle router bit, and base
oper.):

Parts to be oiled (5 hours):　Shaper elevating mechanism, and fence

Parts to be waxed (1 hour):　Shaper table, fence, and miter gauge, router base

Date	Hours of Operation	Maintenance Notes

**Because both tools are so similar in principle, the maintenance schedule for
the shaper can be made to include the router.**

SHAPER ASSEMBLY AND INSTALLATION

Normally there should be no assembly required with the shaper; these machines are usually assembled at the factory before they are shipped to the distributor. New or used, it is always a good idea to check each part against the schematic to make sure that everything is in place and tightened down properly. Among other things, this will help familiarize you with the working parts of the tool.

SHAPER AND ROUTER MAINTENANCE

My maintenance schedule for the shaper includes a section for the router (page 69). Where the router will not require as much maintenance, the tools are similar enough that they can be grouped together. In that way I am reminded to check my routers each time the shaper is cared for.

The shaper has a drive belt which should be checked both for condition and tension. There should be just enough tension so that the belt does not slip. The elevating shaft, bevel gears and column should be kept clean and free of sawdust. These mechanisms are normally enclosed behind an access door within the base (right). After cleaning, oil these parts with SAE 20 machine oil. I clean and oil these parts after each five hours of use. At the same time, make sure that the fence adjustments operate freely and are kept clean.

The router has a much simpler means of setting the depth of cut. The separate base assembly slips over the router body and then locks down once the depth has

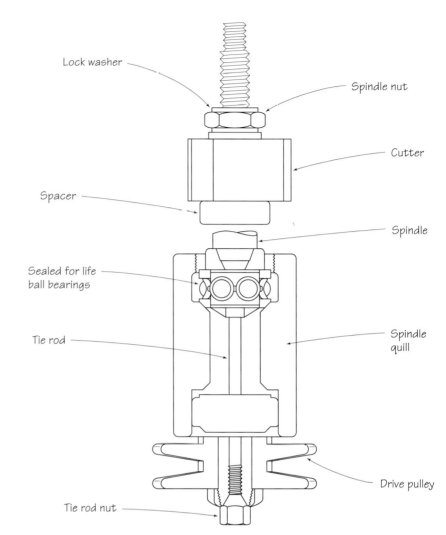

The operating mechanism, which includes the elevating shaft, bevel gears and the spindle assembly, should be free of dust and well oiled.

been set. This adjustment area should also be kept clean and should be well oiled after each five hours of use. The power cord should be checked periodically, especially where it enters the body of the router. These cords take a lot of abuse and should never be wrapped around the tool when it is stored.

SHAPER LOCATION

The shaper is not part of the "golden triangle" of operation. In the ideal shop situation, it should

be placed away from walls with plenty of room all the way around. It should also be placed away from the table saw, radial saw and jointer (top page 71). Again in the ideal situation, this tool should be anchored to the floor in some manner. If the situation is not ideal, a stabilization plate similar to the one shown with the table saw on page 14 can be used. The usual caution line should be painted in the area of operation or around the perimeter of the stabilization plate.

SHAPER DUST COLLECTION

There is a very important dust collection port that is part of the fence assembly (botto right). This exhausts the chips while the machine is operated with the fence on. A considerable amount of suction is required to ensure that the chips do not collect between the fence and the work. It is recommended that a separate dedicated collection system be used for this machine. When the fence is not employed it is not necessary to use the vacuum or dust collector.

SHAPER AND ROUTER ADJUSTMENT AND ALIGNMENT

Although the mechanical shaping tools are simple in concept, there are constant adjustment and alignment procedures that must take place. The shaper spindle and router base must be adjusted for every setup. The shaper fence must be adjusted around the knives and also for depth of cut. Spacers, rub collars and collets must be reconfigured and changed to accommodate all types of operations. Some shapers and overhead routers have angle adjustments that allow the cutter to shape at an angle (top page 72).

Shaper Adjustment

Except for some industrial types, shapers and routers are very typical in appearance. Once you have set up, adjusted and used one of these tools, you should feel confident using any other make or model. In other words, you could probably read any good operational manual to learn how to make these adjustments on your particular tool.

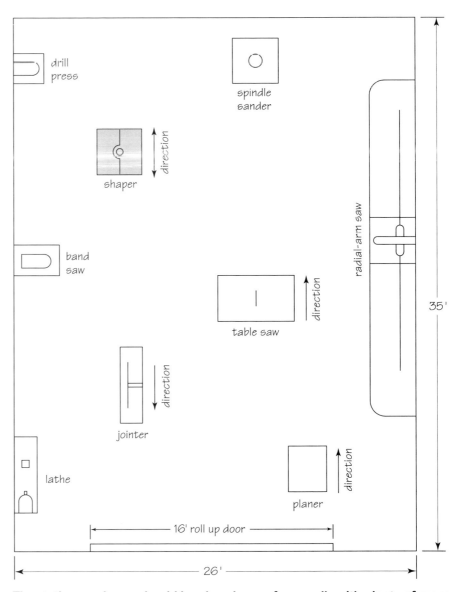

The stationary shaper should be placed away from walls with plenty of room all around.

Most shaper manufacturers design a dust collection port within the fence assembly. Note the flexible vacuum hose, which allows the fence to be adjusted.

Adjustments

1. The height of the shaper spindle or router base for depth of cut adjustments.
2. Changing the cutters on the shaper, or the bit on the router.
3. The fence on the shaper, which should be parallel to the miter gauge slot.
4. The router guide (or fence), for controlled inside cuts.

Alignment

On the shaper, the spindle is part of an assembly that mounts directly to the bottom of the table. If the table or cutter assembly does not have an angle adjustment, the spindle should be exactly perpendicular to the table. With the cutters and spacers removed, this should be checked with a small square at several places on the table (right). The same is true for the router: If the collet assembly, which holds the bits, is not square to the router base, there is a major alignment problem. This can be checked on the router by installing a straight fluting bit and using a square, as with the shaper. If a problem does exist, chances are that the shaper spindle assembly is loose where it meets the table, or the router base is not tightened down properly.

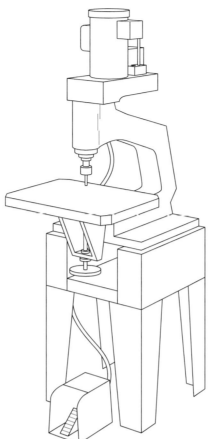

Some industrial shapers and overhead routers have a means to change the spindle angle. This is an additional adjustment and alignment concern.

A square is used in several locations around the spindle to check that it is square with the table.

SHAPER AND ROUTER PARTS

The Shaper Fence

The two-part shaper fence can be adjusted in many ways. The space between the two fence halves can be made larger or smaller, depending on the cutters that are installed on the spindle. This space is adjusted to be as minimal as possible. Loosen the screws that hold the two wooden fence halves and adjust them toward or away from the cutters. There should be about ⅛"-¼" clearance between the fence ends and the widest part of the cutter (top right).

The fence can be adjusted to allow more or less of a cut depending upon the cutter and setup. This is always adjusted parallel to the miter gauge slot in the table. The two fence halves must be 90° to the table and in line with each other (bottom right). If, after checking with a straight edge, the fence is not in line, it may be necessary to use shims or replace the wooden fence halves. Once straight, one half of the fence can be adjusted in a parallel, offset position to accommodate jointing procedures, etc. (top page 74).

The Router Brushes

If properly cared for, there is not a whole lot that can go wrong with the router. A very high speed tool (20,000 to 28,000 rpm), the motor brushes can wear quickly. Per the maintenance schedule these brushes should be rotated after each five hours of actual use (bottom right). This will keep the brushes wearing evenly and extend the life of the router.

There should be ⅛"-¼" of clearance between the adjustable shaper fence and the cutter. This adjustment is made after loosening the screws that hold the two wooden faces to the fence.

When shaping less than the whole surface, the shaper fence should be kept in line with a straight edge.

Shaper Cutters and Bits

There are three kinds of cutters used on a shaper. The one-piece, three-wing cutters are considered safest. These cutters are ground to shape on the back side in a way that honing the flat face does not alter their shape (top page 75).

The three-knife safety cutterhead is much the same as the moulding head that is used on the table or radial arm saws. Although the diameter of the head is smaller, the same knives that are used in the moulding head set can be used in the shaper cutterhead.

The clamp-type cutterhead uses two knives and is considered the most dangerous. The knives are clamped down within the cutterhead in a way that they could work loose if not set up properly. Only experienced journeymen capable of grinding their own knives should use this type of cutter.

Router Bits

Two basic types of bits are used in the router. The one-piece bit has the shank built right into the two-wing cutter. Some of these bits have a pilot or removable bearing wheel that follows the edge of the work. The removable wheel can be changed to achieve a specific horizontal depth of cut.

The interchangeable router bit is built of separate cutterheads, shanks and roller bearings. The shank (or arbor) is threaded into one side of the cutter, and a roller bearing is threaded into the other side if needed.

All of the cutters for the shaper and bits for the router are offered in selected high-grade steel or with carbide tips. In today's rapidly growing and competitive tool mar-

When joining the entire surface, the fence should be adjusted to an off-set position. Note that the two fence halves are still in line.

The router motor brushes should be rotated regularly to keep them wearing evenly.

ket, the more desirable carbide types are not that much more expensive than steel. Each type can be maintained by honing the flat face to keep a sharp cutting edge, but the steel type will dull much faster. If you elect to hone your own bits or cutters between professional sharpenings, be sure and do all of the faces equally. This is especially important on the three-wing shaper cutters. If not honed equally, the wings will be of slightly different length. This will cause balance problems, which will result in uneven, chattered, cuts.

CLEANING, OILING AND WAXING

Except for some portable models, the shaper is usually an enclosed tool. Clean out the sawdust from the operating mechanisms regularly. After they have been cleaned, the elevating shaft, bevel gears and column should be oiled. The fence should be kept oiled at the point where the two halves adjust for the offset (bottom right). The table, fence faces and miter slide should always be waxed before operation.

The air vents on the router should be kept free of sawdust by blowing them out regularly with compressed air. The bottom of the collet assembly should be cleaned regularly so that it does not keep the split collet from tightening around the router bit. The ball bearings on the motor shaft are permanently grease sealed, and no further lubrication is necessary. Once properly cleaned, the moulded subbase, which rides on the wood surfaces, should be waxed.

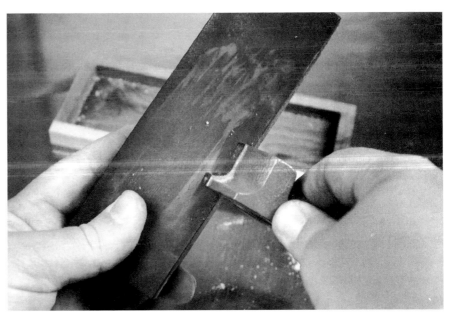

Honing the flat face of the cutter will maintain a sharp edge. Be sure that all wings are honed evenly.

The two-piece shaper fence should be kept clean and oiled at the point where it is adjusted for the offset.

The Shaper and Router Troubleshooting at a Glance

1. The shaper work or router kicked back

PROBLEM	SOLUTION
Wrong feed direction	Always feed opposite the direction of cutter rotation

2. Burn marks on wood or cutter

PROBLEM	SOLUTION
Dull cutters	Have cutters professionally sharpened or hone the flat side of each wing
Wrong feed direction	Always feed opposite the direction of cutter rotation

3. Work hits shaper outfeed fence

PROBLEM	SOLUTION
Fence halves are not in line	Align the fence halves with a straight edge (make sure that both pieces are 90° to the table)

4. No support after wood passes shaper cutter; snipe or gouge at end of cut

PROBLEM	SOLUTION
Fence misalignment	Adjust the outfeed fence to compensate when entire edge of stock is removed
	Align the fence halves with a straight edge if only part of the stock edge is removed by cutter

5. Depth of cut not uniform

PROBLEM	SOLUTION
Shaper spindle or router base not tightened down enough	Tighten properly

PROBLEM	SOLUTION
Shaper or router bit pilot loose or digging in	Use ball bearing pilots (whenever possible) and tighten them properly

6. Cuts not smooth

PROBLEM	SOLUTION
Cutter dull or honed unevenly	Sharpen cutter properly
Wrong speed	Use higher rpm if possible (shaper only)

7. Excessive chips between the shaper fence and work

PROBLEM	SOLUTION
Exhaust problem	Clear exhaust port and check vacuum system

ALL OPERATIONS (BOTH TOOLS):

✔ Cutter or bit is sharp and tightened down
✔ Fence aligned and tightened down
✔ Shaper spindle or router base depth is locked
✔ Direction of cut noted
✔ Guard and holddowns in place (if applicable)
✔ No obstructions on or around the tool
✔ Appropriate surfaces are waxed
✔ Safety glasses on

FOR THE SHAPER:

✔ Vacuum is in place if fence is used
✔ Taper pin is in place if pattern shaping
✔ Miter slide is in place if cross shaping

FOR THE ROUTER:

✔ Cord has plenty of length and out of the way
✔ Work to be shaped is held down properly

CHAPTER SIX

The Surface Planer

The surface planer is a specific tool. Used to reduce the thickness of rough or preplaned lumber, it excels in this function like no other tool. While some surfacing can be performed with certain sanding machines or the jointer, there are limits and size constraints with these tools. A well-tuned planer will mill a board or panel of any length to a uniform and consistent thickness. The milling will be limited to the maximum width of the specific machine. As a rule, the wider the planer, the larger the planer.

When I started out in woodworking, a surface planer was something that was seen only in the larger cabinet shops and mills. Considered to be an industrial tool, there were just a few larger models on the market. Nowadays, planers are offered in a variety of sizes and from many different manufacturers. Competition in the market has forced the prices down so that even the weekend woodworker can afford to own one.

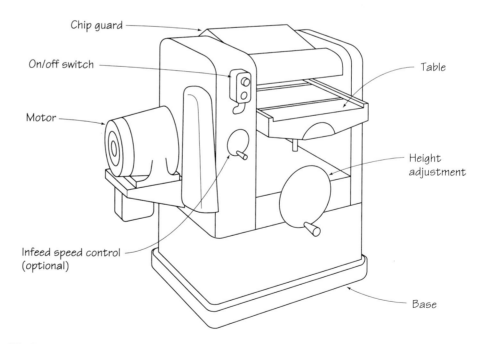

Chip guard

On/off switch

Motor

Infeed speed control (optional)

Table

Height adjustment

Base

All planers have the same basic function and components. Regardless of the manufacturer, this would be a typical surface planer anatomy.

The dust collection system will attach to the housing located at the top of the planer. It will be necessary to run the exhaust system from above.

Spacewise, some models have become so compact and light that they can even be stored under the workbench until needed. Of course these smaller models are not capable of running thousands of board feet at a time, but they will sure serve efficiently within their own parameters.

TYPES OF PLANERS

In a nutshell, the planer is comprised of an adjustable table, a cutterhead and a feed mechanism all assembled on a stand that houses the motor (page 78). Unlike the jointer, the cutterhead works from above the work. The length of the cutterhead, which holds from two to four knives, determines the size of the machine; anywhere from 12 to 20 inches would be a typical size planer for home or small professional shop use. The table will adjust up or down via a rotating handle. This adjustment determines the depth of the cut. The table can be adjusted to accommodate any gauge of material, usually up to 6″ thick. The self-feed mechanism, also working from above the work, is controlled via a gear reduction system, which is driven from the same motor that works the cutterhead.

PLANER SAFETY

The surface planer can be a very dangerous tool. There are many things that should be considered before operating this high-speed piece of equipment. As I always point out, good maintenance is the best way to stay in touch with all of your tools. This will help to eliminate the possibility of accidents occurring due to mechanical failure, which is 50 percent of the safety battle. The other 50 percent has to do with understanding the machine and knowing how the lumber will react to the feed roller, chip breakers and planer knives.

The chip guard/cutterhead cover must always be in place before the planer can be operated. Without this cover, the knives would be exposed and there would be no protection against the high-velocity chips the cutterhead produces. This cover is also the area of exhaust to which a vacuum or dust collector should be connected (above). Every major manufacturer offers an adaptor that will fit over the chip guard for this purpose. Beyond these concerns, be sure to read the owner's manual and understand the limitations of your specific planer. With these limits in mind, and an operational checklist tacked up close by the planer, there will be little room for error.

Safety Rules

- The planer will not flatten twisted or cupped lumber. (In this situation, one side of the stock should be jointed flat before it is passed through the planer.)
- The work piece should be supported beyond the outfeed table.
- Surface stock with the grain turned in the right direction.
- Always stand to one side of the planer, and not in line with the stock.
- Never feed the material into the planer against the grain.
- Always release the board once the feed rollers take hold.
- Never plane a board that is too short. The board should be 2″ longer than the distance between the infeed and outfeed rollers.
- Always allow the machine to come to full speed before feeding the stock.
- Never surface used, dirty or painted lumber.
- Always lower the bed and turn off the power if a board gets stuck in the machine.

PLANER ASSEMBLY AND INSTALLATION

The planer is one of those stationary tools that come to the consumer assembled from the factory. They may require some simple tasks such as mounting the body to a stand or adding table extensions, but for the most part this is a self-contained tool. In any event, the machine should be checked thoroughly for any loose parts, shipping clamps or alignment problems before it is operated for the first time. Scrutinize every part of the machine while checking it against the schematic in the owner's manual. This will also help familiarize you with each part and how it functions.

There are many different designs available today, including small, portable machines used for light-duty operations. There should be some thought given to supporting the work piece on each side of the machine. As mentioned above, table extensions are available for most planers, but some of these smaller models do not have this feature. A "dead man" or home-built outfeed table is always a good idea if long stock will be planed. The extension, table or dead man should be set at an angle that is slightly higher than the back bed. This will guard against an annoying "snipe" that may occur when the stock leaves the front feed roller.

PLANER MAINTENANCE

After initially checking the machine, prepare a maintenance schedule specific for the planer (page 81). This should note the serial number, date of purchase and any parts that should be changed, oiled or greased. For the most part, the planer is a belt-driven tool. There is usually more than one drive belt involved due to the tremendous friction created by the cutterhead. It is a good idea to keep an extra set of belts on hand at all times in the event one breaks prematurely. These belts should be changed once a year or more often if necessary. The knives will

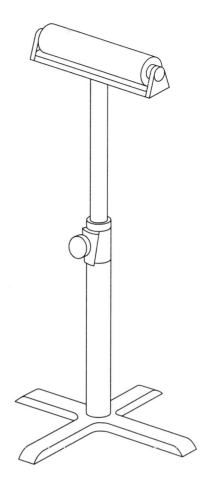

If there is no one available to help "catch" the lumber on the finished end, use a table or "dead man" to support the weight. This will avoid any end "snipe."

Surface Planer
Maintenance Schedule

Serial Number:

Date of Purchase:

Parts to be aligned (5 hours):   Table, bed rollers, upper rollers

Parts to be oiled (5 hours):   Elevating mechanisms, feed gears and chains, feed roller bearings, cutterhead bearings

Parts to be waxed (1 hour):   Table top, exposed elevating worm gears

Date	Hours of Operation	Maintenance Notes

Make a maintenance schedule similar to this that will be specific for your planer.

have to be changed and sharpened when they become nicked or dull. There are chains associated with the gear reduction feed system that must be oiled frequently. Beyond these things, I clean and lubricate all moving parts after at least each five hours of use. Be sure to include the date on the schedule each time the machine has been serviced in any way.

LOCATION OF THE PLANER

For permanent installation in a cabinet shop, the planer should be placed on the opposite side and behind the table saw, as is the jointer. The planer is large and heavy, but it is still a good idea to bolt it to the floor. There is a lot of vibration associated with this tool, not to mention the feeding action of the lumber, which will tend to move the machine in time. A caution line should be painted on the floor in front of and behind the machine—at least four feet in each direction.

Portable or stationary, be sure that there is plenty of room at each end to accommodate whatever length of material you intend to plane. My planer is situated close to a roll-up door, which gives me an infinite amount of room in the one direction without taking up valuable shop space. There should also be enough room on each side to allow the operator to walk around and "catch" the lumber as it leaves the back bed.

PLANER DUST COLLECTION

As previously mentioned, the dust collection port is located in a metal piece that attaches to the chip breaker on top of the machine. This necessitates that an overhead exhaust tube be designed. There

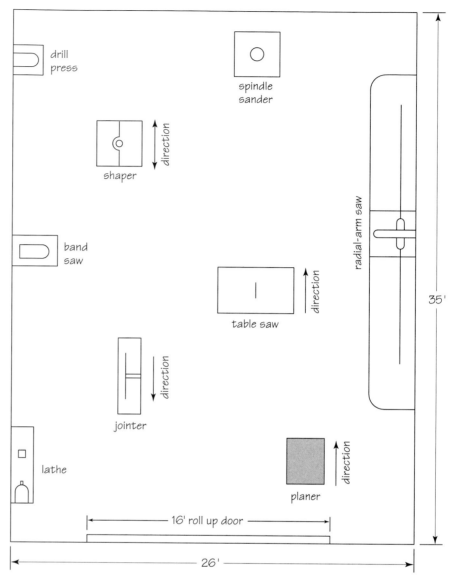

In the ideal situation, the planer should be placed on the opposite side of the table saw than the jointer. Leave enough room both in front and behind for the longest length you intend to plane. Note the proximity of the roll up door for added feed length.

is a tremendous amount of waste associated with this machine, so a simple shop-vac will not do. I recommend that this tool be connected to a separate exhaust system not in line with the other tools, especially if you intend to do a lot of planing. The switch should be located close to the planer, but the actual unit can be situated outside the building somewhere.

PLANER ADJUSTMENT AND ALIGNMENT

The planer is built to withstand a lot of shock and vibration that is created by the friction of surfacing wide lumber. At times this tool is used to its full capacity, when the entire widths of the knives are in contact with the wood. There are many moving parts that are controlled either by manual adjustment, friction, or by a motor that has more than one function. The table moves up and down either by manual adjustment or, in some cases, by the motor. The cutterhead is running at full speed (up to 8,000 rpm) and the upper rollers are gear-reduced to a much slower feed rate. The bottom rollers work from the friction of the material that passes over them. A typical planer has an infeed roller, outfeed roller, a cutterhead and two bottom rollers (top).

The kind and amount of controls depend on the size, design and manufacturer of the particular planer. Regardless of how elaborate the machine, all planers will have the same basic functions. Read your specific owner's manual to learn how to make these adjustments.

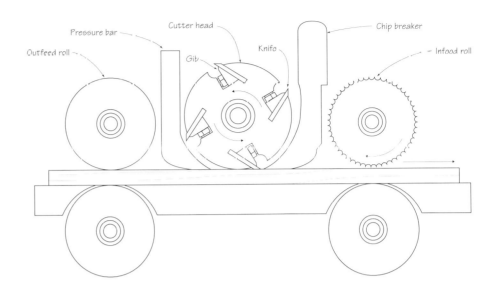

Most medium-size planers have two upper and two lower rollers. The chip breaker and pressure bar surround the cutterhead.

To check that the table is parallel to the cutter, plane a separate piece at each end of the table. The pieces should be the same thickness once planed. Use dial calipers to measure thickness.

Adjustments

1. The table (or bed) vertical adjustment
2. Bed roller adjustment
3. The feed rate (not all planers have a feed rate adjustment)

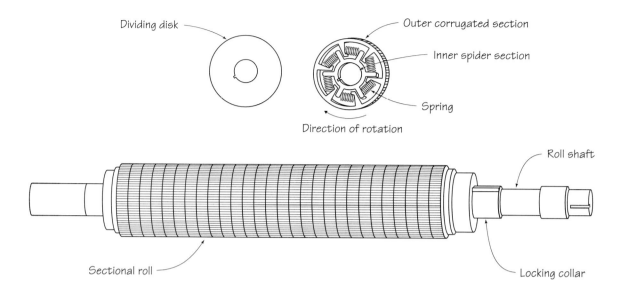

Dividing disk

Outer corrugated section

Inner spider section

Spring

Direction of rotation

Roll shaft

Sectional roll

Locking collar

Most striated in-feed rollers are sectional. This allows material of slightly different thicknesses to be fed evenly through the planer.

PARTS OF THE PLANER
The Table

Regardless of the elevating system, the table should always move up and down smoothly and parallel to the cutterhead. Most planer tables work on a four-post worm gear system. Each corner has a means of adjustment that will make it possible to align the table and regulate the "slack" or "drag" on the post. Check to make sure that the table is parallel by planing two separate pieces of 2"-wide stock, one on each side of the table (bottom page 83). Once planed they should be the same thickness. If the pieces are not parallel, an adjustment is in order. Check your manual to see how this adjustment will be made.

The elevating mechanism, which is connected to the handle, should be well oiled and turn freely. If there is too much drag, the table will tend to bind. Conversely, if the table is too loose on the posts it will vibrate, causing chatter marks on the work surface. This is a fine-line adjustment that will require some trial-and-error

testing. Be sure that the worm gear mechanism is well oiled and dirt free before beginning this adjustment. A dry or dirty elevating gear can cause a drag condition that is not related to the post adjustment.

The Bed Rollers

Most planers have two bed rollers mounted into the table. These occur in front of and behind the cutterhead. The rollers work from the friction that is created by material being fed from the upper motorized rollers. The bed rollers can be adjusted by a lever or set screws under each end. It is important that each roller be straight and true. If a roller is bent it will manifest itself by a stop and go, or jerky, action. If a bent roller is suspected, remove it from the bed and roll it along a flat surface to verify the problem. If your suspicions are correct, the roller must be straightened or replaced.

Ideally, the rollers should be at a different height from the table for rough lumber than they would be for lumber that has already

been surfaced. This distance is measured by first lowering the bed, disconnecting the power, and then placing a straight edge across each end of both rollers. Check with an automotive feeler gauge at each end of the straight edge. For rough stock there should be about .015" at each end of the straight edge. For pre-surfaced stock this distance should be about .005". For planers without a "quick change lever," a good medium height would be .010".

The Infeed Roller and Chip Breaker

The infeed roller is the means by which the stock is moved toward the cutterhead. This roller is located in front of the cutterhead, and is usually made in sections (above). The entire roller is slightly striated so that it is able to grab the wood. The sectional aspect allows pieces of slightly different thicknesses to be run at the same time along different points of the cutter width. Tension on this roller should be great enough that it ac-

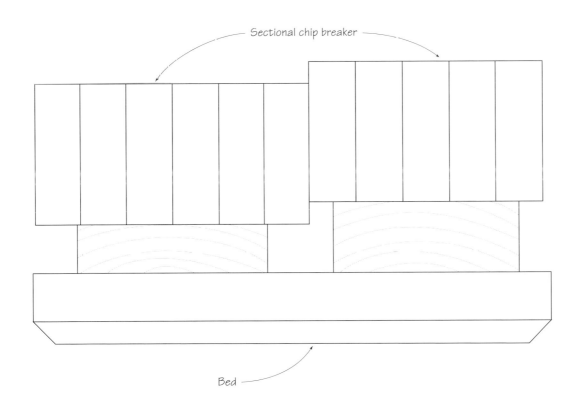

Sectional chip breaker

Bed

The chip breaker keeps the wood from tearing. It should be set even with the bottom of the cutter apex.

tually depresses lines into the wood, which will ultimately be removed by the cutter. The tension should not be so great that the lines still appear on the finished piece. This tension is adjustable from under the cutter guard, per your owner's manual.

Like the infeed roller, the chip breaker is usually made in sections (above). This part is located close to the knives, and keeps the wood from tearing upward. Working in conjunction with a pressure bar, which is at the opposite side of the cutter, the chip breaker also keeps the work pressed firmly down to the table. Both of these devices should be adjusted even with the bottom of the knives' arc, close to the material being milled. This is an important adjustment. If the chip breaker and pressure bar are too high the material will vibrate and have a rippled effect. If the pressure bar, which is located on the outfeed side of the knives, is too low, it will bind the material, and possibly mark up the newly planed surface.

The Cutterhead and Knives

The cutterhead is cylindrical and holds two, three or four knives, depending on the design. The accuracy of the cut depends on the cutterhead bearings, and all of the knives being sharp and set at the same height. Bad bearings in the cutterhead will be evident by the annoying knocking sound they make when the machine is turned on. If bad, the bearings will have to be replaced, or they will only get worse. There should not be any play between the cutterhead and bearings.

Planer knives should always be sharpened professionally. Some manufacturers offer an attachment for their planers that allows the knives to be "jointed" in place. It is also possible to lightly hone the beveled side of the knives by hand (with the power disconnected) while they are still in the cutterhead. This can not be done too many times before it begins to round the knives. If the knives become prematurely chipped, they can be slightly offset from each other, as with jointer knives, in an effort to gain a little more life.

There are many ways to install the knives. Depending on the manufacturer, a jig is usually provided specific for the planer design. Installation procedure is very similar to the jointer, except that the knives are referenced to the cutterhead instead of the table. Most newer planers have a simple means to elevate the knives into position underneath a "crows foot" type of device that rests on the cut-

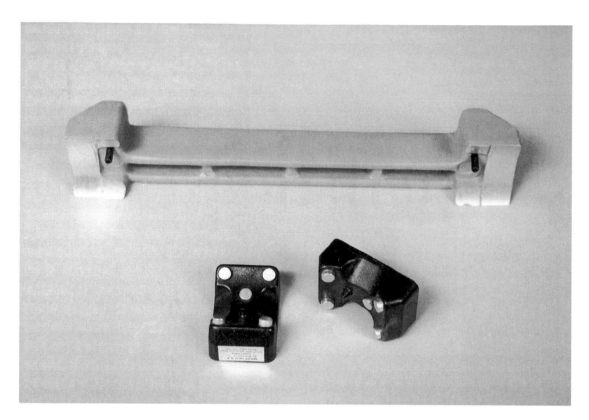

Most planers are supplied with a "crow's foot"-type jig for setting the knives. The knives are referenced from the cylindrical planer head.

terhead (figure 6-11). If your planer is older or you do not have a jig for setting the knives, there are a variety of magnetic jigs on the market that are made just for this purpose. Be sure to blow out and clean the knife gibs and spaces before installing the new knives.

CLEANING, OILING AND WAXING

All of the moving parts require constant cleaning. Blow the exposed parts off frequently with compressed air to remove the dust. Each time the knives are changed or serviced and the cover is off, blow off and clean the "hidden" parts. It is a good idea to remove the pulley cover at this same time to make sure that this area is also clean. Remember that dust and dirt are abrasive and have a clogging effect on gears and pulleys. Lacquer thinner on a rag works well for cleaning these parts.

Oil all gears, chains and moving parts frequently. Wax, instead of oil, is recommended on the elevating worm gears if they are exposed; this will keep the dust from clinging to these parts. Naturally, the table should be kept waxed at all times. I like to use stick paraffin for this purpose because it is a little heavier than paste. Rough lumber tends to wear the wax off quickly in any event, and the paraffin is quick and easy.

The Surface Planer
Troubleshooting at a Glance

1. Boards are tapered across the width

PROBLEM	SOLUTION
Table is not parallel with the cutterhead	Make the appropriate adjustment to one side or the other, per the adjustment section of this chapter
Bed rollers are not set parallel with the table and cutterhead	Check the bed rollers with a straight edge and feeler gauge on both sides of the table
The knives are not set evenly in the cutterhead	Check the knives with the jig provided or with a magnetic jig

2. Washboarding effect on newly planed surfaces

PROBLEM	SOLUTION
The knives are dull or not set at the same level as each other within the cutterhead	Check that the knives are sharp and that they are all at the same height within the cutterhead
Depth of cut may be set too deep or the table needs waxing	Take several shallower passes and/or wax the table

3. Stock stops or hesitates in the machine

PROBLEM	SOLUTION
The pressure bar or chip breaker is set too low	Reset the pressure bar and/or chip breaker level with the bottom of the cutter's apex
The bed rollers are set too low or the table needs waxing	Adjust the bed rollers to .010″ from the bed and/or wax the table

4. Planed surfaces are chipped

PROBLEM	SOLUTION
The exhaust system may be full or not strong enough to exhaust the waste	Empty the vacuum and try again; if the vacuum is not strong enough, upgrade
The chip breaker is not set correctly	Reset the chip breaker per the owner's manual

5. Either end of the board has a snipe

PROBLEM	SOLUTION
The pressure bar or chip breaker is set incorrectly	Reset the pressure bar and chip breaker per the adjustment section of this chapter and the owner's manual
Pressure bar spring tension may be too light	Check the pressure bar springs and replace them if necessary

6. Indented lines across the width of the board

PROBLEM	SOLUTION
Striated infeed roller is set too low	Check the infeed roller depth and tension and adjust if necessary

Surface Planer

ALL OPERATIONS:

✔ Table is set to proper depth
✔ The material is turned for grain direction
✔ Vacuum is engaged
✔ Dead man support in place for long stock
✔ Table is waxed
✔ No obstructions around the planer
✔ Safety glasses on

CHAPTER SEVEN

The Drill Press

The drill press is, in my mind, a somewhat underestimated tool. Many other operations beyond the simple drilling functions can be performed. Of course, many of these do require the use of attachments and jigs, but the fact remains that this is a tool with many capabilities. Depending on the particular drill press, the additional functions include routing, sanding, shaping, mixing, mortising and lathe work.

Primarily used for the precision drilling of all kinds of holes, the drill press is a stationary tool. Unlike the use of a portable drill motor, the work is brought to the machine. This affords the ability to use an array of bits that can drill at any predetermined angle. This tool has a variable-speed capability via either a dial/cone pulley or manual belt/pulley adjustment, which enables the tool to be used for many mediums, including wood, plastic and metal.

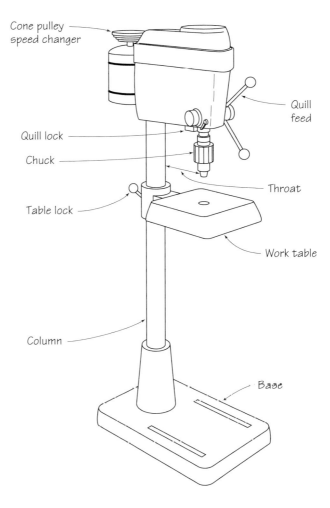

Cone pulley speed changer

Quill feed

Quill lock

Chuck

Throat

Table lock

Work table

Column

Base

In spite of any manufacturing variables, a typical drill press will have these basic components. The difference between floor and bench models may only be the length of the column.

TYPES OF DRILL PRESSES

There are a multitude of types and sizes when it comes to selecting a drill press. Height, speeds available, power and angle selection features are some of the variables that should be considered. In spite of these variables, all drill presses will have the same basic components. There will be a tool head, which houses the motor, quill and quill feeding apparatus. This is connected by a column to an adjustable table and some sort of heavy base. The difference between the floor and bench models may only be the length of the connecting column the work table slides on. The size of the machine is usually determined by the throat distance from the column to the center of the chuck.

There are three main functions to this machine which, used in combination, will allow for the many setups that the tool is capable of. First, the speed may be changed according to the material being milled and the size of the drill bit being used. Second, the quill, which holds the drill chuck, can be made to extend via the quill feed, or can be locked into a fixed position for sanding and shaping operations. Third, the table can be adjusted vertically and, in many instances, can be tilted to a specific angle. The radial drill press has an added feature that allows the head to both extend and tilt.

DRILL PRESS SAFETY

Beyond the usual underlying and common sense safety concerns associated with power equipment, the drill press does have its own set of rules. As I point out with all of the tools, good maintenance plays

Some drill presses will have a rack fixed to the column and a gear lever at the back of the table. This is just a simple means of adjusting the height of the table.

an important role in safety. The work space itself also lends to, or diminishes, the chances of getting hurt or hurting others. Do not underestimate the dangerous potential of this machine.

The drill press does not have any type of factory guard. This would lead one to believe that it is not a dangerous tool. Unfortunately, I have seen a lot of accidents occur in school workshops because the operators have let down *their* guard. One of the most common things that happens has to do with long hair that is not tied back. The drill bit and chuck are quite unforgiving when it comes to snagging anything that they come into contact with. I will not let anyone in my class approach this tool with loose hair or clothing.

As simple as it may seem, the drill press is as potentially dangerous as any of the circular saws, planers, or shapers. Read your operational manual to gain understanding. Keep a checklist close to the tool to remind you of safety.

Safety Rules

- Check the speed reference for drill size and type of material being milled.
- Do not force the press faster than the material will allow.
- Be sure that the table hole is lined up with the bit or that there is a buffer board under the work.
- Always unplug the tool when changing the belt, making adjustments to the motor or changing pulleys.
- Never operate with long hair or loose clothing.
- Always make sure the work is held or clamped securely to the table.
- Never start the tool with the bit lowered onto the work.
- Always make sure that the chuck is tightened securely around the bit, and remember to remove the chuck key.
- Never operate the tool without wearing safety glasses.

Drill Press
Maintenance Schedule

Serial Number:

Date of Purchase:

Parts to be aligned (3 hours):   Pulleys and belt, spindle and chuck (checked for runout), table, quill
                                 lever

Parts to be changed (1 year):   Belt

Parts to be oiled (5 hours):   Quill lever and shaft, column (split pulley if dial controlled)

Parts to be waxed (1-2 hours):   Table

Date	Hours of Operation	Maintenance Notes
		•

**A maintenance schedule similar to this should be designed specifically for
the drill press.**

DRILL PRESS ASSEMBLY AND INSTALLATION

Before a drill press can be operated, it must be properly assembled. Often this tool comes from the factory in a number of boxes. The head (which includes the quill, spindle, chuck and pulley guard) will already be assembled and will have to be attached to the column and base. The work table will mount to the column, which may have a gear rack fixed to the side (page 90). Each design is a little different, so follow the instructions carefully. If the head does come preassembled, be sure and check it thoroughly against the schematic for any loose screws, pulleys or other mechanisms. The motor may come separately and have to be mounted to the head. In any event, the belt will always have to be tightened properly between the drive and driven pulleys.

As previously mentioned, the only difference between a manufacturer's floor and bench models may be the length of the column. If this is the case, and the bench model is what you have purchased, you may want to buy an auxiliary floor model column. The space in your shop may only allow for a bench model most of the time, but it is nice to have the versatility of the floor model for those certain jobs that require a longer distance under the chuck. It's something to think about!

MAINTENANCE

As with all of the tools, I recommend that you make a maintenance schedule specifically for the drill press. As always, this should include the date of purchase, serial number and all of the parts to be

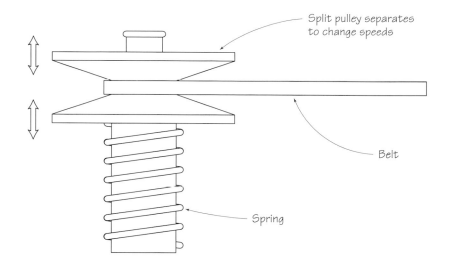

Split pulley separates to change speeds

Belt

Spring

A variable-speed drill press employs the use of a dial-controlled split pulley system for speed control. The split pulley changes size, thus changing the speed.

The best way to check for spindle runout is with a dial indicator or calipers. The chuck should be checked with a straight metal dowel. If there is more than .015″ deviation, the spindle should be checked and repaired if necessary.

oiled, changed and maintained (page 91). The drill press is a belt-driven tool, so it is a good idea to keep an extra belt on hand. I change mine once a year without fail, but sometimes they wear, tear or break unexpectedly, so it is nice to be prepared.

With the drill press, I clean and lubricate all of the moving parts, including the chuck mechanism, after each five hours of operation. It is a good idea to clean the column with some 0000 steel wool and lacquer thinner at the same time, and to apply a light machine oil to allow the table to move freely. I always note the date and approximate running time on the schedule each time the maintenance is performed.

DRILL PRESS LOCATION

The drill press is a machine that is easy to place. Even the floor model does not take a lot of room, and can be placed along any wall or in a corner. The bench model can be set on a rolling cabinet or, as the name implies, anywhere on the workbench. The fact that this tool does not require a direct vacuum system adds to the ease of placement.

DRILL PRESS ADJUSTMENT AND ALIGNMENT

The drill press is a very simple concept. The spindle and chuck should run true, and the speed at which it turns should relate to the material being milled. The size and type of bit used will also dictate speed. There is an adjustment stop associated with the quill feed lever that governs the depth of cut. The quill feed lock knob allows the quill to be locked into place at any

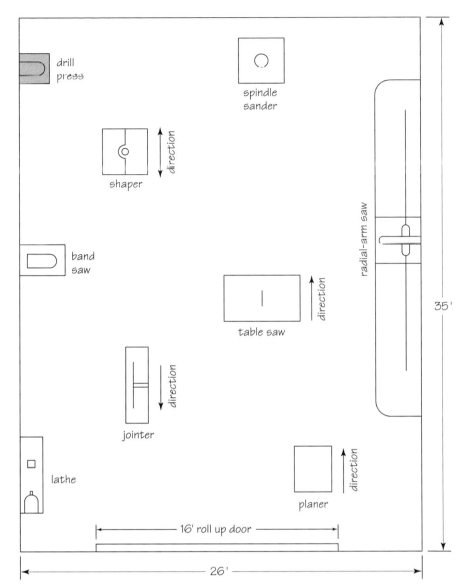

The drill press is not part of the golden triangle and can be placed near an out of the way corner.

desired depth within the throw distance. Table adjustments include the vertical and sometimes angular movements along the column.

Adjustments

Although there are size and type differences, the basic components will always remain the same. After going through the initial assembly check, and setting up your maintenance schedule, you should have a feel for the components. Check your owner's manual to see how these adjustments will be made.

Adjustments

1. Spindle speed. The speed will be governed by either a dial/split pulley (top page 92) or a cone/step pulley (bottom right).
2. Table height and angle adjustment. The table will have a locking handle and means by which it can be raised or lowered. (Not all drill presses have a table angle feature.)
3. Quill feed and lock. All drill presses have a feed lever and a means to lock the quill at a desired height.
4. Depth stop. There will be a means to govern the quill feed depth.

Alignment

The first and foremost consideration will be to check that the spindle and chuck are running true. The best way to check for runout is with a dial indicator (bottom page 92). Not everyone has one of these at their disposal, and it is an expensive luxury if you are not in business. Another way to check the spindle is by clamping a piece of square metal stock to the table, and using a feeler gauge (top right). Use a short, straight piece of metal dowel held securely in the chuck. Clamp the square stock to the table with the end not quite touching the dowel. As you rotate the spindle via the pulley (by hand), you can measure any difference between the dowel and square stock with the feeler gauge. Any more than 0.015″ deviation may be cause for concern.

An alternate method of checking runout is to mount a dowel in the chuck, clamp a piece of wood to the table, and place a thin metal rule between the wood barely touching the dowel.

The pulleys must be in line to guard against premature wear and tear. The belt should be level with the head of the drill when it is on the same level of both pulleys.

DRILL PRESS PARTS
Chuck

If there seems to be a problem with runout at the chuck, remove it from the spindle. Check the owner's manual for instructions on how the chuck would be removed on your machine. Once removed, you can check the spindle directly with the same square stock/feeler gauge method. This will tell you if the problem lies within the spindle or the chuck. If the spindle is the culprit, there may be a quill/bearing problem, and it may have to be replaced. I might add that this is a rare problem with a new machine, and is only a problem if you are having trouble drilling "true" holes after trying several different bits.

Pulleys and the Belt

Speed is governed by the step or cone pulleys within the head of the drill press. If yours is a step pulley system, you need to check that the motor pulley and driven pulley are in line. Begin by arranging the belt or belts on the same level across the pulleys (bottom page 94). At this point the belt should be level with the head. If not, it will be necessary to adjust one pulley or the other until they are level. The importance here has to do with stress on the belt and making sure that the belt does not rub on the pulley guard. This could cause premature wear to the belt, pulley, motor or the cover itself. Once you are comfortable that the pulleys are in line, the belt should be tensioned properly. Tension is usually set by moving and locking the motor to a desired position.

If yours is a variable-speed machine, the speed will be set with a dial. The variable-speed changer is

The quill feed lever is the means by which the spindle is lowered. Be sure that the quill lock is not engaged when trying to use the feed lever.

an arrangment of two-piece pulleys (top page 92). The sides will open or close as you adjust the dial. This will change the size of the pulleys, and hence the speed of the drill. This type of pulley system must also be in line to operate efficiently.

Feed Lever and Depth Stop

The feed lever will lower the quill to a desired level within its "throw range" (page 95). This must operate smoothly at all times. There will be a locking mechanism that allows the quill to be locked to a depth within the throw range. Be sure that this lock is backed off when not in use. If you feel drag on the feed lever, it is either from lack of oil or the lock being partially employed. The lever should return automatically to the 0 position by the use of a spring within. This tension is also adjustable, and should never be so great that the lever returns with a "bang."

The feed can be limited to a specific depth by the use of the depth stop (top right). This stop is usually located outside of the head, near or as a part of the feed lever. To set the depth stop to a desired position, first raise the table so that the work piece will be slightly under the bit. Lower the bit to the desired depth using a scribed line on the edge of the work piece as a guide (bottom right). At this point, lock the quill in place and adjust the nuts on the depth stop. Once the quill is unlocked, the feed lever will return to 0 and can only be relowered to the depth that was set.

The Table

The table is adjustable to height and sometimes angle. The normal operating position of the table is 90° to the spindle and chuck. This should be checked with a square against a straight rod clamped in the chuck (top page 97). Check at several positions around the table to be sure that the rod is at 90° all around. This is especially important if the table is angle adjustable; if this is the case, set the angle indicator to 0° once 90° has been confirmed.

The Bits

There is an array of drill bit configurations typically used in the drill press. These include twist bits, brad-point bits, forstner bits, spade bits, multispur bits and adjustable bits. All of these should be sharpened professionally. There are some inexpensive twist drill sharpeners on the market that do an ex-

The depth stop governs the feed depth. This should be preset to the desired depth before work is begun.

Once the work table has been adjusted, the feed lever can be lowered and locked into position according to the line that has been scribed onto the edge of the work piece.

cellent job of keeping this type of bit keen. Otherwise, it is probably not cost effective to have the smaller twist bits sharpened at all. The only type of drill bits that should not be used in the press are bits with a screw point (bottom right). These are self-feeding and could destroy a work piece or cause an accident.

CLEANING, OILING AND WAXING

The column, table and chuck require constant cleaning. Lacquer thinner applied with 0000 steel wool or a rag works well for this process. After cleaning, apply a light oil to the column, chuck and quill feed mechanism to keep them moving freely. Be careful not to get the oil on the table or quill clamps. If your drill press has a radial adjustment on the table, some oil will be in order on the pivot area. The table itself should be waxed frequently and after each time it is cleaned.

The work table is at 90° to the spindle during normal operation. This should be checked with a square at several positions around the table.

DANGER! The only kind of drill bits that should not be used on the press are screw-tip bits. These are self-feeding and work against the machine.

The Drill Press
Troubleshooting at a Glance

1. Drilled hole is not true

PROBLEM	SOLUTION
Spindle or chuck has too much runout	Check runout on both the spindle and chuck; if either is more than 0.015″ variation, take necessary measures per alignment section

2. Bits seem to overheat, causing burn marks

PROBLEM	SOLUTION
Bit is dull	Sharpen or replace the bit
Spindle speed is incorrect	Check the speed chart for type of material and bit size speed recommendations

3. Drilled holes are not 90°

PROBLEM	SOLUTION
Table is not at 90° to spindle	Square the table to the spindle in several places and correct accordingly

4. Belts break frequently

PROBLEM	SOLUTION
Belt tension on the pulleys is too great	Check the tension on the pulleys each time the belt is replaced
The pulleys are not in line with each other	Check the pulley alignment

5. Preset depth changes inadvertently

PROBLEM	SOLUTION
Depth stop nuts are not tightened properly	Reset the depth and tighten the nut (install a lock nut if necessary)
The table is not locked into position	Realign the table and make sure that the table clamp is secure

6. Chuck slips or slows down

PROBLEM	SOLUTION
Drive belt is loose or worn	Remove the pulley guard and tighten or replace the belt
Incorrect speed	Refer to speed chart for possible faster speed

Drill Press

ALL OPERATIONS:

✔ Speed is set correctly
✔ Bit is tightened in the chuck
✔ Chuck key is removed
✔ Table is set to the proper height and locked
✔ Table angle is set and locked if necessary
✔ Depth stop is set if necessary
✔ Quill depth lock is not engaged unless necessary
✔ There are no obstructions around the press
✔ Safety glasses are on

CHAPTER EIGHT

The Lathe

I have saved the most creative and fun of the stationary power tools for last. Often thought of as a luxury item, this tool can be very versatile and is multifunctional. With the use of a few accessories, the lathe can become a disc sander, buffer, grinder, trim saw or a horizontal drill press. Creatively, this machine can open many doors and help to turn an otherwise ordinary project into something original. It is highly recommended to read all that you can regarding the use and operation of this versatile piece of equipment.

Primarily used to produce cylindrical and rounded parts of many types and configurations, the lathe is fairly simple in concept. There is a driven center which, in conjunction with a tailstock, allows for the turning of spindles, columns, bases, etc. The headstock is also made to accept a face plate that is available in several diameters. This plate can mount either on the inside or the outside of the driven head and is

Lathe face plates are available in different diameters (normally 3″ and 6″) and are used either on the inside or outside spindles.

used to hold the stock while working on edge and inside turnings such as plates and bowls. A variety of chucks and screw centers are also available to hold smaller pieces while turning such parts as knobs and finials. In all of these situations the work is held in a fixed, but rotating, position. The cutting tools are moved by hand across the tool rest, or sometimes automatically across the surfaces being cut.

TYPES OF LATHES

While conceptually all the same, lathes do vary in size from the small home-shop models to very large industrial types. A medium-size lathe is capable of turning up to 36″ in length and up to 12″ to 14″ in diameter between the headstock and tailstock.

The lathe can be described as having a bed, or ways, on which a driven headstock and moveable tailstock are mounted. The tailstock is adjusted according to the length of piece to be turned. There is also a tool rest, which is typically mounted onto the bed, between the centers and under the work. Auxiliary stand-mounted tool rests can be purchased or made to serve while working from the outside arbor or when doing very large turnings between the centers.

The main functions that require adjustment include the tailstock, which moves laterally across the bed, and the tool rest, which is itself adjustable for height and angle. The delivered speed of the arbor is adjusted via a manual cone (or step) pulley or a variable-speed handle that controls a split pulley. The speed at which the headstock arbor turns is an important function. This adjustment could be

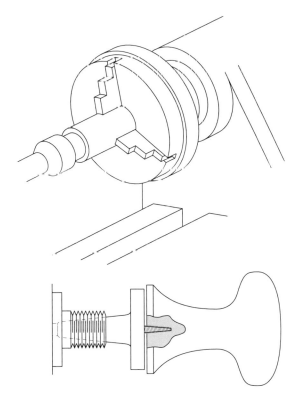

A variety of chucks and screw-type centers are available for use on the inside spindle. These are used when the tailstock is not employed.

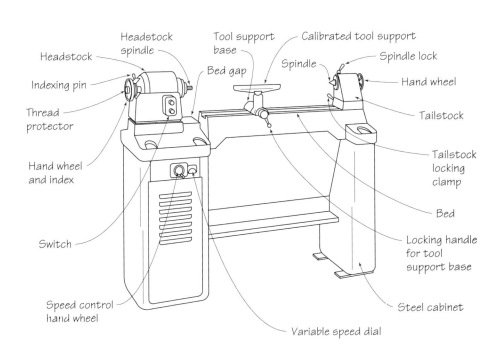

Although lathes are available in many sizes and configurations, they all will have the same basic components. This would be the typical anatomy of a medium-size lathe.

made several times during a single turning for the different stages of cutting and sanding. Naturally, there would be additional adjustments to be made according to any accessories that are mounted to the basic machine.

LATHE SAFETY

Because the lathe is simple and fun to operate, it is easy to become relaxed while using it. It can be dangerous to lose respect for the moving parts and other potential hazards. Strict attention must be paid to every step—from installation of stock to removal of product. Naturally, if the tool is well maintained there is less chance of mechanical failures that could cause accidents. A well lit and clutter-free work area also contributes to safety. After eliminating these common-sense precautions from the equation, good operating habits and technique can become the area of focus.

There are two guards that should be used when operating any lathe. The upper pulley guard protects the operator from the moving drive belt, which is close to the live center and near the area of operation (figure 8-4). A lot of accidents have happened when this guard was not in place. The second guard protects the operator from the flying chips produced while carving a moving object. A plastic shield that covers the upper half of the machine replaces the face shield that must otherwise be worn. This chip shield is made to pivot in the back and fold up out of the way when the machine is not in operation (bottom right).

Read your owner's manual and any operational handbooks that

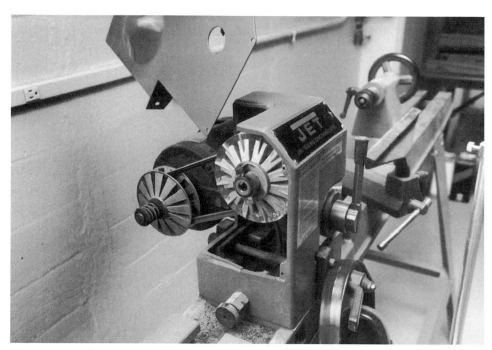

The upper pulley guard protects the operator from the drive belt and pulley. Many accidents have happened when this guard was not in place.

Some newer model lathes come equipped with a plastic chip guard. These are made to pivot in the back and protect the operator from flying chips during operation.

you can to gain an understanding of the lathe before you ever operate one for the first time. Beyond that, you should keep a copy of the checklist printed at the end of this chapter close to the lathe. This operational checklist will help remind you of the particular safety concerns associated with this tool.

Safety Rules

- Be sure that the speed is adjusted according to the size and type of work being turned.
- Make sure that the tailstock and tool rest are locked down.
- Keep the tool rest ⅛" above center at all times.
- Always remove loose jewelry and tuck in any loose clothing or hair.
- Never have the tool rest more than ½" away from the piece being turned.
- Always rotate the part to be turned by hand before switching to power.
- Never operate the lathe without the pulley guard and either a chip guard or face mask.
- Always use sharp chisels, which require less pressure on the work piece.
- Never place your hand between the work and the bed (on large diameter turnings) while sanding.

ASSEMBLY AND INSTALLATION

Consisting of a stand, motor and bed assembly, a new lathe usually

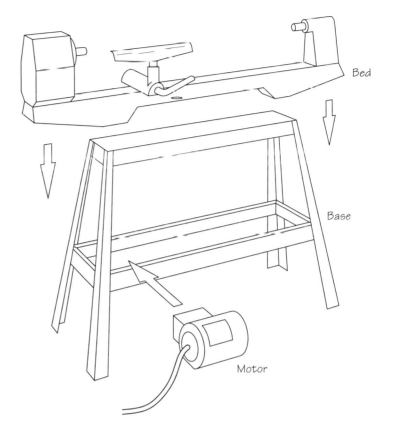

Most new lathes will have to be assembled. The basic components include the stand, the lathe bed and the motor.

needs to be put together when delivered from the factory. This is just a matter of bolting the stand or base together and installing the motor and bed per the manufacturer's instructions. Lathe bases are made to be extra strong due to the vibrations associated with turning. Be sure that all of the bolts are completely tightened down and that any bracing or gussets supplied by the company are installed in the appropriate places. Once assembled, the stand will be ready to accept the motor, which is usually mounted below, and the lathe bed. Again, when mounting these parts make sure that all nuts and bolts are tightened down, and use lock washers whenever possible, even if they are not supplied.

LATHE MAINTENANCE

After assembly, it is a good idea to make yourself a maintenance schedule specific for the lathe. As always, this schedule should note the serial number, date of purchase and any parts that must be periodically changed or oiled (page 104). Regardless of whether the speed is changed by a variable-speed dial or manually, the lathe is always driven by a belt. Because drive belts are made of rubber, I change mine once each year so that they do not surprise me in the middle of a project.

The live (or driven) arbor bearings are usually sealed for life and do not require additional lubrication. The tailstock has no bearings to oil, but the distance adjustment,

Lathe
Maintenance Schedule

Serial Number:

Date of Purchase:

Parts to be aligned (3 hours):   Pulleys, center points, tool rest base clamp

Parts to be oiled (5 hours):   Dead center retraction, motor (if needed)

Parts to be waxed (1-2 hours):   Bed or ways, tool rests

Date	Hours of Operation	Maintenance Notes

The maintenance schedule for the lathe should include the serial number, the date of purchase and any parts that need to be replaced, oiled or maintained.

which moves in and out, should be lubricated after every two to three hours of use. The top of the bed, or ways, should be waxed often so the tailstock glides easily across when installing or removing parts. Oiling the bed is not a good idea because of the dust that is produced.

By its very nature, the lathe generates an abundance of wood chips and sawdust. If the motor is not enclosed, it will have to be blown out often with compressed air. If air is not available, a vacuum will serve. Be sure that the chips and sawdust are at least cleared with a whisk broom, and never allow them to pile up past the motor vents. Beyond the routine cleaning of the tool, be sure to note any maintenance on the schedule along with the date that it was performed.

LATHE LOCATION

Permanent installation of the lathe in a furniture or cabinet shop should be against a wall, and can be out of the way of the golden triangle tools. Because this machine is accessed from the front, or down side of rotation, it can be placed within two feet of the wall. There must be just enough room to get behind the tool for cleaning and maintenance purposes. Whether the floor is made of concrete or wood, the lathe base must be bolted down. This is a tool that sets up vibration, especially when the material is being roughed out. If the floor is concrete, be sure to use some type of lead, or expandable sleeves and lag bolts, in all four corners.

Once installed, a caution line should be painted on the floor two

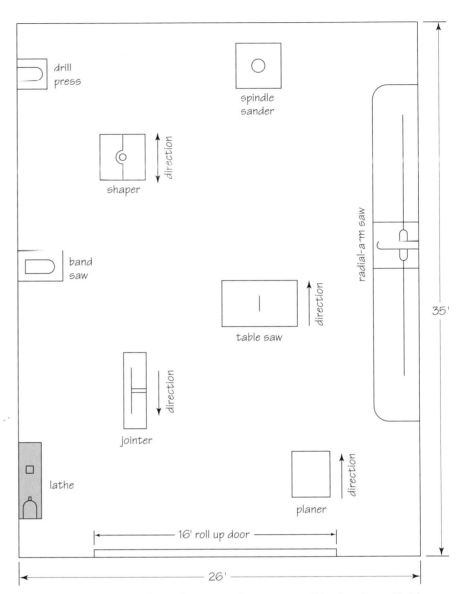

The lathe can be placed two feet away from any wall in the shop. Not important to many projects, it can be located away from the golden triangle of operation.

to three feet out from all three exposed sides. This line should remind both the operator and others in the room that the tool can be dangerous during use. Caution lines also define the space around a tool so that it is less prone to collect clutter. These lines should be painted in red or yellow and swept clean so they can be seen.

LATHE DUST COLLECTION

There are no dust collection ports associated with the lathe. It is a

free and open tool that creates a lot of waste in the area of the turning. If anything should be installed close by, a compressed air bib would be the thing; this allows the actual area of operation to be blown off frequently during the many stages of the turning process. If a compressor is not available, keep a whisk broom handy to do the job. Beyond this, the floor should be swept after each turning is completed, and the waste picked up or pushed into a floor register if a central vacuum system has been installed. A portable shop vacuum is also handy to do a thorough cleaning job once work has been completed.

LATHE ADJUSTMENT AND ALIGNMENT

The lathe has very few moving parts. All of the main functions involve use of the headstock. The hollow spindle, which is threaded on both ends of the headstock, turns at between 900 and 3,600 rpm, depending on the pulley arrangment. The tailstock and tool rest both are movable, but are not always employed. When used in conjunction with the headstock, the tailstock "dead center" must be in direct line with the live, or "spur," center. Variable-speed lathes have a split pulley, which could also be considered as a movable function.

Adjustment

Lathes do differ in size, configuration and capacity, but all have the same relationships and adjustment concerns. In addition to the basic functions, there are a number of accessories available for most lathes (right). Each of those additional items will have a specific set-up procedure. Fortunately, every lathe and accessory will have a means to adjust the components built into the design. Read your owner's manual to learn how the adjustments will be made.

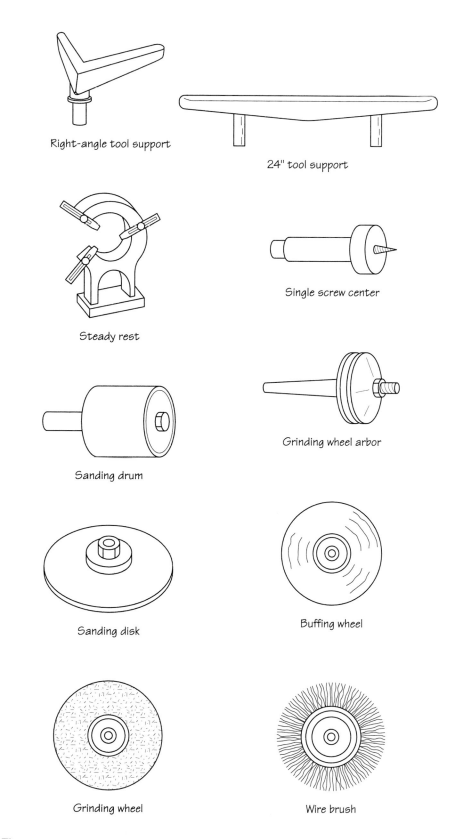

Right-angle tool support

24" tool support

Steady rest

Single screw center

Sanding drum

Grinding wheel arbor

Sanding disk

Buffing wheel

Grinding wheel

Wire brush

There are many accessory items available for the lathe. Some of these can be mounted on the spindles to perform operations other than turning.

Adjustments

1. Speed adjustment and corresponding rpm. The tool will either have a variable-speed dial or step pulley system.
2. Two tailstock adjustments and locks. The tailstock is movable along the bed and has a dead center distance adjustment.
3. Tool rest adjustments and locks. The tool rest base will adjust along the bed, and the interchangeable tool rests will adjust for height and angle.

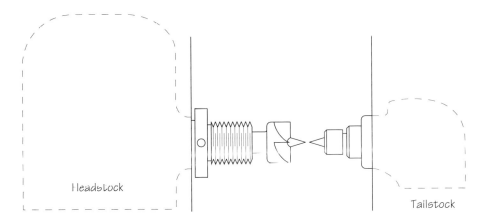

Headstock

Tailstock

The points of both the driven spur center and the dead cup center must line up on both the horizontal and vertical planes. If these are out of line, the turning will not be cylindrical.

Alignment

Every lathe setup, with the exception of outside arbor turnings, will be completed by using a combination of the three relationships just mentioned. The only difference with outside arbor turnings is that a floor stand tool rest would be employed in lieu of the bed-mounted tool rest. Tuning the lathe is quite simple compared to some of the more complicated multifunction power tools. The most important adjustment to be made would have to be the proper alignment of the "live" and "dead" centers used for all spindle-turning operations. Proper tool rest alignment would follow as a close second on the list for several reasons. Tool rest alignment governs both safe operation and efficiency. Pulley alignment is a matter of tool and motor longevity. If the pulleys are misaligned, it does not take long to burn out the bearings in either the headstock or the motor, or both.

LATHE PARTS
The Tailstock

The points of both the spur and dead centers must be perfectly aligned in order to produce symmetrical spindle turnings. The tapered driven spur center, which is held in the hollow headstock spindle, is not adjustable. The tailstock, which holds the tapered cup center, is where all adjustments will be made. How this adjustment will be made differs from make to make, and will be a matter of reading the owner's manual specific for your machine. The important thing is that once pushed together, the points of the centers line up in both the horizontal and vertical planes (above). This alignment is achieved by first pushing the entire tailstock, with the center installed, as close as possible to the spur center without touching it (top page 108). The tailstock should then be tightened down to the bed or ways. It will be immediately apparent if the centers are not in line. This should be viewed from both the top and front of the machine. If not in line, the appropriate adjustment should then be made.

Upon completion of the center alignment, the tailstock clamp-down mechanism should be checked (bottom page 108). Here again, every manufacturer will have a different means to accomplish this. Basically, the entire tailstock will need to be clamped into position on the bed each time that it is adjusted for a different spindle length. If this adjustment is loose, the tailstock will move once cutting begins. If the lathe you are operating has a bed, as opposed to a way system, chances are that the tailstock is clamped into position by a cam/handle. As the handle is rotated, the offset cam pulls the clamp up against the bottom of the bed. If this is the case, there will be a nut-and-washer arrangment at the end of the cam that can be adjusted to the proper position (top page 109).

The third and final adjustment involving the tailstock will be to the spindle extension and corresponding locking device. The dead center spindle is made to extend from within the tailstock so that minute adjustments can be made while turning a spindle. Vibration and friction will cause the dead center to wear deeper into the spindle end as it is being turned. A little helpful hint here is to either put a drop of oil at the end of the center (bottom page 109), or to invest in a ball bearing type of dead center which turns with the work. At any rate, the extension device itself should always be returned to the position closest to the tailstock before the center is moved toward the end of the spindle. If the center is extended too far before the tailstock is clamped into position, the work may vibrate as it is being turned. More importantly, there will not be enough length left to extend if an adjustment needs to be made while the work is in progress.

The Tool Rest

The lathe tool rest and its corresponding base are used in conjunction with every type of turning. Regardless if the work is turned between centers, or with a face plate or chuck, the cutting chisels need to be supported while they are being used. This rest system is comprised of four basic parts: the tool rest base, the base clamp, the interchangeable rest and the rest clamp (top page 110).

The base, which moves along the bed or ways, will pivot to achieve the correct distance from the work. Ideally, the rest itself should be ⅛″ from the work. Because of this, the base and rest are constantly adjusted during the cutting procedure. If the lathe has a bed, chances are the tool rest base will be clamped into position via the same concentric cam/handle that was described for the tailstock. The same rules apply regarding

The first step in lining up the points of the centers would be to push the tailstock (with the dead center installed) as close to the spur as possible without touching it.

Every lathe bed tool rest base will have a means to clamp it into position. Typically this would be achieved through the use of a clamp handle.

the importance of this base not moving once it has been locked down. There is a fine line when adjusting the nut at the end of the cam: The locking handle should release easily enough that the base can be moved with ease along the bed, but at the same time there should not be a lot of play between the lockdown and release positions.

The actual tool rest is interchangeable according to the kind of turning being done. There are several different lengths and configurations available for all types of turning. The rest, once inserted into the base, is adjustable both vertically and laterally; in this way the rest will work in combination with the adjustable base to achieve just about any position needed during the different stages of turning. The height of the tool rest top edge should always be ⅛" above the centerline of the turning (bottom page 110). Once the ever-changing position of the rest is established, it will need to be locked down with the clamp handle.

Speed Changes

The speed at which the work is turning (rpm), is very important in terms of efficiency. Basically, the larger the piece being turned, the slower the speed. Also, there should be rpm changes at each stage of the turning process. When the work is being roughed out it will need to be going slower than when it is being sanded. There are operational charts available (usually in the owner's manual) that will give a suggested reference. After turning a few projects, experience will be your best guide for correct speed.

The clamping pressure of the tool rest base is usually governed by a nut at the end of a concentric cam. There is a fine line of adjustment to where this nut is neither too tight nor too loose.

If using a non rotating dead center on the tail stock, a drop of oil or wax between the center and the wood will help keep friction burns from occurring.

If you are lucky enough to have a variable-speed lathe, these speed changes will be a snap. If this is not the case, speed change will have to be done manually with the step pulley system. With step (or cone) pulleys, it is very important that they both be in line. The motor pulley is the only one that will be laterally adjustable, because the driven pulley will be in a fixed position. As mentioned earlier in this chapter, if the pulleys are not in line it will put tremendous stress on both the motor and the spindle bearings. Once the belt alignment has been established, speed changes can be achieved anywhere along the step pulley system.

CLEANING, OILING AND WAXING

The bed, tailstock and tool rest base require constant cleaning. Once blown off or vacuumed, the parts can be wiped down with lacquer thinner on a rag. The bed or ways should be waxed (not oiled) so that both the tool rest and tailstock will glide across with relative ease. The dead center spindle should be oiled frequently where it retracts into the tailstock. Be sure not to get any oil on the tailstock lockdowns or under the bed where the pressure clamps must hold. Check your owner's manual regarding the motor and the need for oil in the bearings. Most motors have sealed-for-life bearings, but this must be verified.

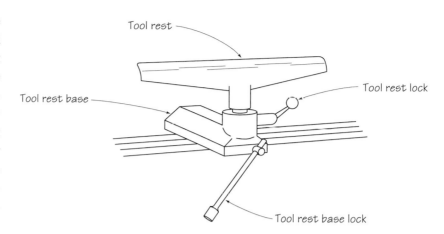

There are four basic parts of the bed-mounted tool rest: 1) the base, 2) the base lock, 3) the interchangeable tool rest and 4) the tool rest lock.

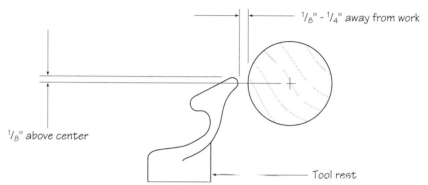

The top of the tool rest should always be ⅛" above the centerline of the turning. This will allow the tools the maximum angle of attack for cutting.

The Lathe
Troubleshooting at a Glance

1. Work is not cylindrical after being turned

PROBLEM	SOLUTION
The points of the spur and dead centers do not line up both vertically and horizontally	Move the tailstock close to the spur center, and adjust per your owner's manual
Cutting tools are not sharp	Always work with sharp tools

2. Machine vibrates excessively

PROBLEM	SOLUTION
Incorrect speed	Refer to operational speed chart; if in doubt, slow the machine down
The machine is not bolted to the floor properly	Check that floor bolts have not come loose

3. Work burns at dead center

PROBLEM	SOLUTION
Tailstock adjustment is too tight or a drop of oil is needed on the center	If the spindle will not rotate by hand, it is too tight; if this is the case, back off on the tailstock pressure

4. Tools grab or do not cut properly

PROBLEM	SOLUTION
The tool rest is too far, or at the wrong height; from the work	Adjust the tool rest and be sure that it is tightened down

5. Work slips between centers while being turned

PROBLEM	SOLUTION
Tailstock clamp is loose	Remove the tailstock and tighten the clampdown mechanism
The spur center was not driven deep enough	Remove the turning, drive the spur center deeper, and re-chuck between centers

6. Lathe hesitates or does not rotate once switched on

PROBLEM	SOLUTION
The spindle turning is too tight between the centers	Release pressure on the tailstock

Lathe

ALL OPERATIONS:
✔ Both guards are in place
✔ Tool rest is positioned properly and locked
✔ Lathe bed is waxed
✔ There are no obstructions around the lathe
✔ Face mask is on

SPINDLE TURNINGS:
✔ Tailstock is properly positioned
✔ Both tailstock locks are employed
✔ Drop of oil on dead center

FACE PLATE TURNINGS:
✔ Work is properly mounted to face plate
✔ Face plate is tightened on the spindle

CHAPTER NINE

Sanding Machines

I have always been of the mind that the sanding process can make or break the beauty of a project. It is the most important process, given good construction, of the furniture or cabinet business. I have seen things that are built well, and then for some reason the ball was dropped in the final process of preparing for the finish. Cross-grain scratches, scratches left from a previous grit, circular marks left from a sander with metal edges exposed to the work piece: These types of things should all be unacceptable to any woodworker. A bad sanding job may be due to a lack of knowledge about the sanding machines or poor maintenance of the tools themselves.

This chapter is of course devoted to sanding machines, large and small. I will mention many different

The portable belt sander is one of the most important tools in any cabinet or furniture shop. The two most common sizes are 3″ × 21″ and 4″ × 24″.

types of sanders in this introduction, some of which are industrial oriented. For the purpose of this book, I will confine my adjustment segment to just a few sanding machines that would be most common in the home shop or small cabinet business. Beyond that, it is recommended that anyone wishing to excel in woodworking gain some knowledge of how sanding is accomplished in industry. It can only help!

TYPES OF SANDING MACHINES

There are drum sanders, stroke sanders, wide (or endless) belt sanders, edge sanders, moulding sanders, pneumatic drum sanders, backstand sanders, scroll sanders and pearson sanders found in industry. These types all take up a lot of room, and for the most part perform specific functions. None of these machines will complete a sanding job from start to finish, but they will all make short work of their particular aspect of the job.

Even large industrial concerns will use some of the same sanding tools that you or I use. Regardless of whether one piece or a hundred are made, the sanding process remains the same. The sanding tools that we all could find a use for are: the portable belt sander (page 113), the oscillating or vibrating pad sander (top right), the spindle sander (bottom right), the stationary (vertical/horizontal) belt sander (page 115), and the disc sander (page 116). These are the few that I will go into detail about, for they are the mainstay of finish woodworking.

The sanding process in general is a series of refinements from one

The oscillating pad and random-orbit pad sanders are used in the final stages of sanding. Available in several sizes, they are capable of sanding against the grain.

A real up-and-coming tool, the spindle sander can sand both inside and outside curved edges.

type of sander to another. The means through which this process is accomplished is always a little different, depending upon the job at hand. The type of sander and paper grit used are dictated by the material and construction of the piece being sanded. There are varying opinions about the sanding process itself, but there is one truth to which all agree: Well maintained sanders will always do a better job.

SANDING SAFETY

Even though sanders do not employ the use of blades, knives or bits to do their cutting, they are still considered cutting tools. Certain sanders are as dangerous as saws or planers. Due to their high speed, the belt and disc sanders have a lot of potential to do harm to the human body: Do not take these tools for granted. The high speed and close tolerance between tool body and moving parts, coupled with the abrasive grits used, can be a formula for disaster.

There are no guards to speak of with these tools. One must always pay attention to the sanders at all times while they are in operation. For instance, it is not uncommon for an operator to "run over" the power cord with the belt sander while looking up for an instant. This can cause electrical shock or a fire in the workshop. The disc and belt sanders have both been known to remove flesh or, even worse, the finger of a haphazard individual. Always use common sense and respect the sanders for what they are—indiscriminate machines.

The stationary belt sander has two positions: vertical for sanding edges and horizontal for sanding faces.

The disc sander comes in several sizes. The most common sizes are 12″ and 14″ in diameter.

SANDER ASSEMBLY AND INSTALLATION

For the most part, portable sanders are ready to go. Some belt and pad sanders do require very light assembly, which includes the installation of base plates and clips. These are very simple procedures that don't take a lot of time or know-how. All of the sanders require that the paper or belts be first installed and then changed as needed. This becomes a matter of procedure as one gets to know the tool.

The larger stationary sanders sometimes do require assembly, especially the stationary belt sanders. Naturally, this is due to the fact that they are large once assembled, and easier to ship in pieces. Each manufacturer is a little different in their approach to packaging. So whatever the type or make of sander that needs to be assembled, just follow the instructions, and check each part as it is installed. Pay particular attention to how the tracking adjustments are supposed to work on belt sanders. Other than these adjustments, make sure that everything is tightened down and oiled well as you assemble it. If you do run into trouble, remember that most manufacturers have 800 hotlines for troubleshooting and assembly questions or problems.

SANDER MAINTENANCE

For the stationary sanders, it is best to make a maintenance schedule that is specific for each tool (page 117). These are considered individual machines with their own sets of adjustments and requirements. As usual, these schedules

Stationary Sander
Maintenance Schedule

Serial Number:

Date of Purchase:

Parts to be aligned (3 hours): Table and angle indicator, Pulleys and belt, top tilt drum, belt position

Parts to be oiled (5 hours):   All pivotal points

Parts to be waxed (1-2 hours): Table tops and miter slide

Date	Hours of Operation	Maintenance Notes

Each stationary sander should have a maintenance schedule specific for the machine. This would be a typical sander maintenance schedule.

Portable Sanders
Maintenance Schedule

Belt Sander
Serial Number:
Date of Purchase:

Large Pad Sander
Serial Number:
Date of Purchase:

Small Pad Sander
Serial Number:
Date of Purchase:

Date	Hours of Operation	Maintenance Notes

**All of the portable sanders can be grouped into one maintenance schedule.
In this way nothing will be forgotten.**

should include serial numbers, dates of purchase and all parts to be maintained. You should even note how often sanding belts and papers are changed; this information will help you diagnose uneven-wear problems that may occur due to worn parts or misalignment.

I like to group all of my portable sanders into one category for maintenance purposes. This schedule can have each sander listed on the one sheet (page 118). It is best to set aside the time to service all portable sanders at once, unless there is an emergency with a particular machine. In this way nothing will be overlooked, because all of the information is on the one sheet.

With all of these tools, I clean and lubricate the moving parts at least after each four hours of use. Sanders are unique in the sense that they create fine dust by their very nature. This dust is extremely abrasive to the moving parts and needs to be cleaned out more often than some of the other tools. Be sure to note the date and what was done each time that maintenance is performed.

STATIONARY SANDER LOCATION

The placement of stationary sanders is strictly a matter of convenience and preference. Some of these sanders do not take up a lot of floor space, and can be tucked in a corner or against a wall some where where they are most needed. Others are large and need to have a specific placement according to their usage and size. Each shop situation is a little different, and sometimes the need for

It is not a good idea to wrap the cords around portable sanders. This puts strain on the cord where it meets the tool body.

efficiency will take precedence in terms of placement.

The portable sanders are a little easier to deal with. These only require a safe place under the bench or in a cabinet when they are not being used. I keep all of my sanders together in one place that is centrally located in the shop. The important thing here is that they are always accounted for and easy to get to wherever a project is being worked on. Try not to get in the habit of wrapping the cords around the machine (above); it is better to "coil and loop" the cord (top page 120).

SANDER DUST COLLECTION

Most sanders, stationary and portable, come equipped with a vac-

uum bag or a vacuum port. This is obviously a very important aspect of the sanding process. If you can not see what you are doing because of the dust in the air, it defeats the purpose. Of course, the larger stationary sanders should be hooked into a main, or specific, vacuum at all times during operation. I also have a large C.F.M. exhaust fan located within the wall of my shop. This keeps the air moving at all times and clears any sawdust, which may escape the vacuum or dust bag, from the air.

SANDER ADJUSTMENT AND ALIGNMENT

All sanding machines are fairly simple in terms of moving parts. With the belt sanders, the belt itself should track correctly and not rub on any edges of the tool body. The disk sander must run true with a minimum of clearance between the disc and adjustable table. The spindle sander must travel up and down smoothly and true to the table. The pads of all oscillating sanders should be flat and free of dirt or grit before the paper is applied to them. Also, make sure that there are no screw heads protruding above the pad level; these will transfer through the paper and mark the surface being sanded.

There are many different makes and models of sanders on the market today. Besides all of these, there are several types of sanding attachments which can be outfitted onto other woodworking machines. For instance, my table saw often doubles as a disc sander when I am producing mitered corners for frames, etc. By substituting an abrasive disc for the blade, I can take advantage of the well-aligned saw table and miter slide to produce perfect miters of any angle quickly and easily (bottom). There are drums and other attachments available for the drill press that will turn this machine into a kind of overhead spindle sander that can make short work of many contour sanding jobs (page 121). These are just a couple of examples of how your other machines can be outfitted to work as sanders. Each of the specific sanders will have the means to adjust components built right into the tools. Read your owner/operator's manual to see how these adjustments are made.

A much better method of storing portable tools is by using the "coil and loop" method of wrapping the cords.

Often other woodworking equipment can double as sanding machines. Here is an example of using a table saw as a disc sander.

Adjustments

1. Stationary Belt Sander
   - How the table to belt angle adjustment will be made. (The table is at 90° to the belt during normal operation.)
   - How the belt tracking adjustment will be made.
   - How the belt and housing are changed from a vertical to a horizontal position.
2. Disc Sander
   - How the table to the disk angle adjustment will be made. (The table is at 90° to the disc during normal operation.)
3. Spindle Sander
   - How the table to the spindle angle adjustment will be made. (The table is at 90° to the spindle during normal operation.)
   - How the spindle size will be changed.
4. Portable Belt Sander
   - How the belt tracking adjustment will be made.
   - How the belt change or tension release is made.

Another example of a tool doing double duty as a sander is the drill press outfitted with a sanding drum.

STATIONARY BELT SANDER ALIGNMENT

As mentioned, the basic relationships of this tool are threefold. On most stationary belt sanders the belt and its housing are capable of being moved from the normal vertical position to a horizontal (or flat) position. The work table, which has a miter slide groove milled into the surface, is capable of tilting for angle sanding. The machine will also have a means by which the tracking of the belt is accomplished. This last adjustment is very important to the quality of the work produced. The tracking adjustment is ongoing, as belts stretch after being used.

Belt Position

The belt position adjustment will be made close to the pivot point of the belt housing assembly (right). There will be a lock knob and autostop arrangment per the owner's manual. The tool body will pivot on the base or stand on some sort of circular ways. This pivotal way system must be kept clean and well oiled. There should not be any play within this pivotal area that could affect the tracking of the belt. The belt housing assembly should move freely when the lock knob is released. Be sure to tighten the knob after changing the position of the belt.

Table Position

The table is adjustable for angle sanding when the belt is in the vertical position. There will be an angle scale on the side of the table which will indicate the table angle. The table and this scale are adjusted by first locking the table at 90° to the belt. Do this with a

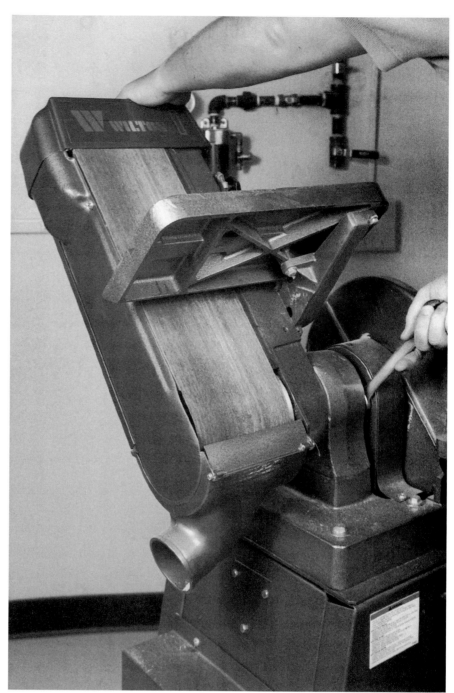

The stationary belt sander has two positions. The lock knob is located close to the pivot point at the bottom of the tool.

square at each side of the belt width (top right). Once 90° has been confirmed, the angle scale indicator can be set to 0°. All other angles can then be set per the scale indicator. Be sure that the table pivot area is also clean and oiled at all times. Each time that the table angle is changed the table lock must be employed. When the belt is in the horizontal position, the table is always set at 90°. In this position the table is acting as a "stop" for what is being sanded.

Belt Tracking

The most typical stationary belt sander sizes would be 4″×36″ or 6″×48″. The belt rotates in a clockwise manner or toward the table. If you look on the inside of the belt there will be an arrow which indicates the direction that the belt should rotate. This is important because the "lap point," or where the belt is glued together, should travel in such a way that the friction of sanding does not work against the seam in the belt. Once direction is determined, release the tension on the upper drum so that the new belt can be slipped on. After the belt has been installed, raise the upper drum until there is no slack in the belt. Do not make the belt too tight on the drums.

The second and most important adjustment will be the tracking of the belt. The tracking is adjusted by tilting the upper drum tilt knob at the top of the machine (bottom right). By turning this knob, the belt will move left or right, depending on the knob's rotation. The machine has to be turned on for this adjustment to be completed. Do this initially by turning

The first step in adjusting the belt sander table is squaring the table to the belt. Once this has been accomplished, the angle scale indicator can be set to 0°.

The belt is tracked by the tilting drum at the top of the sander. The tilt or "tracking" knob is located close to this upper drum.

the power on and off quickly until you are "in the ball park." The belt is tracking properly when it neither moves right nor left, and is in the middle of both the upper and lower drums. Be sure that the tracking knob is locked down once this has been accomplished. As the belt is used it will stretch; it then becomes necessary to increase the tension and retrack the belt.

DISC SANDER
The Table
The disc sander works in conjunction with an angle adjustable worktable. This is located at the center of the disc so that the entire paper surface can be utilized. The table is slotted to accept a miter slide, which is also angle adjustable. These adjustments are made with a square in both directions by first achieving 90° and then setting the scale indicator to 0° (top right). Be sure that the circular ways and pivots are always clean and well lubricated.

Motor and Disc
Basically a direct-drive tool, the bearings on the motor and the arbor shaft are the things to watch. If there is any play in these bearings, the disc will not run true. A bent shaft will cause the same effects, but is easier to correct. If the bearings are bad the motor will have to be rebuilt or replaced. In the case of the belt-driven disc, the pulley alignment and belt tension are important factors. If tension is too loose, the disc can slip and slow down during operation. If the belt is too tight or out of line, there is excessive strain on the arbor bearings.

The most typical disc sizes are

There are two angle adjustments involved with the disc sander. Both the table and miter slide should be first squared to the disc, then the angle indicators can be set to 0°.

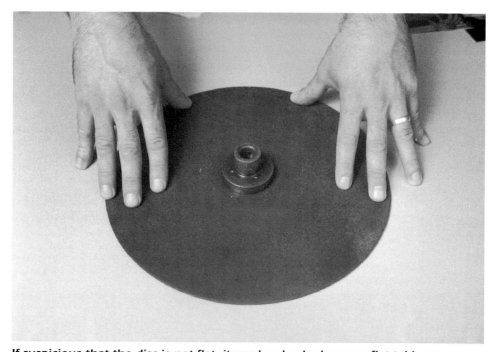

If suspicious that the disc is not flat, it can be checked on any flat table or surface. A disc that is not flat will cause the paper to wear unevenly.

12″ and 14″ diameter. The disc itself must be flat or the paper will wear unevenly and cause the tool to vibrate. If suspicious, you can check the disc on a flat table (bottom page 124). Whichever way the disc is mounted to the drive, it should be adjusted parallel and within ⅛″ to ¼″ of the table leading edge; paper thickness varies according to the grit and weight, so this distance won't always be the same. Too much space will cause smaller work to vibrate or jam. The disc guard, which covers the top 40 percent of the plate, is also adjusted closely to the outside disc circumference. Be sure the face is thoroughly cleaned between paper changes. This also protects against uneven paper wear.

There are many sizes of hand-held disc sanders. These typically come in 4″ to 8″ diameters and have flexible back plates for the sanding disc (top right). This tool is often variable speed, and is used mostly for contour and sculptural sanding. Keep the motor cooling ports blown out frequently because the dust is abrasive and could cause overheating and eventual burnout. The brushes in the motor should be rotated often to keep them wearing evenly.

SPINDLE SANDER

A real up-and-coming tool, the spindle sander is a genuine time-saver for finishing the edges of both inside and outside curves. Unlike the vertical-arbor-held drum sander, the beauty of this machine is that it reciprocates to constantly clear the paper and at the same time use more of the sanding sleeve surface. This up-and-down motion is made possible

Disc sanders can be mounted in a drill motor to become handheld sanders. Handheld disc sanders have a flexible back plate. These are used primarily for contour or sculptural sanding.

The first point of reference on the spindle sander is that the spindle must be 90° to the table. This is checked with a square at several points on the table.

by a gearing system in a sealed reservoir of oil. Be sure that the reservoir is full and the oil is kept clean. There is also an external air port open to the oil. This is covered with a screen that should be kept clean at all times.

The Table

The table, which surrounds the spindle, tilts for angle sanding and has a throat plate hole milled into the surface. The plate that is used in the inset would be the size closest to the spindle surface. A minimum clearance is recommended for the same reasons cited previously. The size of the table is governed by the overall size of the machine. Normally, the table will tilt 45° in each direction. There will be a simple table lock and a scale that will indicate the angle. The spindle should be squared to the table and the indicator set to 0° (bottom page 125); all other angle indications will then be correct. Be sure that all pivotal parts are well cleaned and oiled at all times.

This table size can be increased for certain project applications. The use of an auxiliary table that can fit over the existing table is common with this tool. If used, it is important that this table be flat and well secured. When locating this tool for permanent installation, try to leave access all the way around the table.

THE PORTABLE BELT SANDER

This is one of the key finishing sanders in any cabinet or furniture shop. The typical sizes are 3″ × 21″, and 4″ × 24″. Made to take to the work, the belt sander removes material quickly on flat surfaces. Belt

The tracking knob on the portable belt sander is located on the side of the machine. The belt is tracked by a tilting action of the front drum.

It is important that the thin metal plate between the sanding belt and tool body be flat and clean. Be sure that the clamp screws are tightened down and do not protrude.

tension, mostly automatic, is governed by a spring that should be kept clean and well oiled. As with all belt sanders, direction is indicated by an arrow inside the belt. The tracking is achieved by use of the tracking knob located on the side of the machine (top page 126). This adjustment will tip the front drum so that the belt will move. This process will be an ongoing adjustment, as the belt wears and stretches.

The motor air intake ports should always be blown out and kept clean. Most belt sanders have an exhaust bag that catches the majority of dust. Keep this bag emptied, or the dust may back up on the work. The motor brushes should also be cleaned and rotated per your maintenance schedule.

The thin metal plate between the tool body and sanding belt will wear over time. These are replaceable and should be changed when worn. Be sure that this plate is flat and clean, and that the plate clamp screws are well below the belt (bottom page 126). If too high, these could cause marks on the work as the belt becomes worn.

PAD SANDERS

These sanders are used in the final stages of finish sanding. There are a variety of sizes on the market that take from ⅛ to ½ of an 8 ½″ × 11″ sheet of paper. The high-speed oscillation of the sander makes it possible to sand against the grain. In this way any cross-grain scratches left by previous sanders will be removed.

The clips that hold the paper must be strong enough that the paper does not vibrate loose. These need to be replaced when worn.

The compressible material at the bottom of the pad sander must be in good shape. Any flaws in this pad will cause the paper to wear unevenly.

There is a felt or some other type of compressible material between the paper and metal base plate; this should be cleaned often and replaced when worn (above). If there are motor brushes, be sure to rotate these per your maintenance schedule.

CLEANING AND WAXING

All of the table surfaces should be cleaned with lacquer thinner and then waxed frequently. This allows the work to glide across the surface. Even auxiliary tables should be treated this way. On those tables with a miter slot, keep both this area and the bar of the slide well waxed. The entire machine should always be blown out after each operation so that dust is never allowed to sit. This is also a good opportunity to look the machine over for any loose or worn parts.

The Sanding Machines Troubleshooting at a Glance

1. The stationary belt sander

PROBLEM	SOLUTION
Belt will not stay on track	Increase tension and retrack with tracking knob
Sanded edges are not square	Make sure that belt position is locked and the table is square to belt

2. The disc sander

PROBLEM	SOLUTION
Sanded edges are not square or at desired angle	Make sure that the table is set and locked at desired angle
Sanding or burn marks on work	Paper is worn or disk is not running true

3. The spindle sander

PROBLEM	SOLUTION
Sanded edges are not square or at desired angle	Table is not 90° to spindle or set to the desired angle and locked
Burn or chatter marks on sanded edge	Change to larger spindle size or move paper sleeve to expose less worn sandpaper

4. The portable belt sander

PROBLEM	SOLUTION
Belt is not tracking properly	Adjust the tension spring and retrack belt with tracking knob while the sander is running
Marked depressions on sanded wooden surface	Check that thin metal plate is flat and that plate clamping screws are not too high

5. The pad sander

PROBLEM	SOLUTION
Paper is worn only in certain spots	Check that compressible surface between sandpaper and base plate is flat and has no holes
Paper vibrates off while sanding	Check that paper clamps are tight enough around the paper; if not, tighten or replace them

ALL SANDERS:

✔ Paper is of correct grit and not over worn
✔ Paper is held securely
✔ Table tops are waxed
✔ There are no obstructions around the sander
✔ Safety glasses and face mask are on

STATIONARY BELT SANDER:

✔ Belt position is set and locked
✔ Table is set at desired angle and locked
✔ Belt is tensioned and tracking properly
✔ Miter slide is set and locked

DISC SANDER:

✔ Table angle and miter slide are set and locked

SPINDLE SANDER:

✔ Table is set to desired angle and locked
✔ Correct throat plate is installed

PORTABLE BELT SANDER:

✔ Belt is tensioned and tracking properly

PORTABLE PAD SANDER:

✔ Material between paper and base is clean

CHAPTER TEN

Handheld Power Tools

Every shop, large or small, will have a variety of hand-held power tools specific to the type of work being done. These are the tools we carry right to the projects, and the ones that serve us over and over as the years go by. They are also the tools that take the most abuse; they are kicked across the floor, set in precarious places and dropped more often than any-one cares to admit. We tend to take these time-savers for granted—until they fail us right in the middle of a project. At this point it is realized that there may not be an easy substi-tute for the tool that has always been there.

In this chapter I deal with these marvelous little pieces of equip-ment that often get overlooked when it comes to maintenance. Al-though there are numerous types,

There are three basic sizes of drill motor. The small, high-speed moto-tool (center), the medium-size ⅜" reversible (right) and the large ½" heavy-duty type (left).

makes and models of handheld power tools, I would like to focus on the few most common categories that would be found in every serious woodworking shop. These would have to include the drill motor, the saber saw, the handheld circular saw and the biscuit joiner.

THE DRILL MOTOR

The drill motor would include any device capable of turning at high speed that has a clamping chuck for holding drill bits. These machines range in size from the very small to quite large (page 130). The "moto-tool" is used for carving and for drilling small holes (⅛" in diameter or less). The medium size, and most common, drill for overall versatility is the straight-chucked, ⅜" variable speed/reversible type. The larger sizes are used mostly in rough construction and for metal work. These are drills with ½" chucks and larger.

The drill motor and chuck size are not the only options that need to be considered when selecting the machine for a specific project. In today's market there are also a variety of cordless (or battery operated) drills that are used on-site and during installations where there is no convenient source of power. Then there is the right angle drill, which is used for drilling in tight places or when leverage is needed. Right angle drills are available in all three body sizes.

THE SABER SAW

Originally called the bayonet saw, the saber saw is indispensable when it comes to cutting curves in place. On large pieces that can not be brought to the band saw easily, this saw goes to the work (top

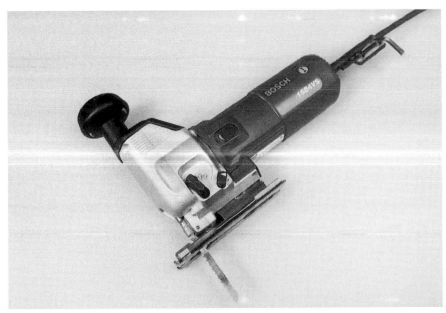

The saber saw is used to cut curves and openings in place or on site when the work can not be brought to the band saw.

The circular saw is a real time-saver for rough cuts in the shop or field. This saw is also known by various trade names.

right). Somewhat limited in the thickness that can be cut, this tool is ideal for a multitude of purposes for materials up to 2" thick. The saber saw is also ideal for keyholing, or cutting openings into countertops and walls. Also capable of cutting at an angle, the base need only be tilted to the desired degree.

Although the blades are interchangeable, there are several sizes to choose from. The size of the saw has to do with horsepower as opposed to depth of cut. Depending on the density of the material being cut, one might want to consider the smaller or larger version of saw. Unlike most saw blades, the saber saw blade is designed with the teeth pointing up, which will always tend to fray on the up-stroke, or the top of the cut.

THE HANDHELD CIRCULAR SAW

The handheld circular saw, also known by some manufacturers' trade names, is a multipurpose tool used both in the workshop and in the construction industry (bottom page 131). This tool operates similarly to the table saw in many respects, but is carried to the work. The size of the saw is determined by the diameter of the blade used. A typical saw uses a 7¼" blade for cutting depths up to 3", but saw sizes range from 6" to 12", according to the particular need. The tool base is adjustable for both depth and angle of cut, and can be used in conjunction with a straight edge (or fence) to produce very precise cuts, rabbets or dadoes. The cutting action of this saw is from the bottom up, thereby producing any fray on the top of the material being cut. For this reason, it is always a good idea to place the best side of the material down. Like the table and radial arm saws, using a carbide blade will help reduce fray.

THE BISCUIT JOINER

A relatively new innovation, the biscuit joiner (above) does a wonderful job of cutting perfectly registered slots for blind splines. This tool makes short work of what used to take hours with the doweling jig and drill bit. The football-shaped pieces used for the actual spline material are available in three different sizes of the same thickness. Made of wood products, these splines are designed to expand

The biscuit joiner is used to cut the slots for blind spline construction. There are three standard spline sizes, all of the same thickness. The tool can be quickly set to accommodate each of these sizes.

once moistened by glue. This machine has the means to set the depth adjustment to accommodate any of the three spline sizes.

Many manufacturers offer their renditions of the biscuit joiner. Although there are stationary versions available for certain production applications, the handheld models are all about the same size. These tools are designed for one function, which they do well. The components include a small circular blade situated within an adjustable spring-loaded base. There are usually two small spring-loaded pins on the leading edge of the base that keep the tool from sliding sideways while cutting.

HANDHELD POWER TOOL SAFETY

I have always taught that particular attention should be paid to the safe operation of handheld power tools: Smaller is not necessarily more

kind. These tools can bite just as badly as the big stationary machines. The fact that they are mobile and there are no guards to speak of makes them just a little more dangerous than their well-guarded big brothers. There are plenty of instances of people being hurt even by the lowly drill motor that has snagged on loose clothing or has slipped from the work piece and into a hand.

For those portable tools with cords, there is the added concern of loose wiring across the floor. It is advisable to hang overhead retractable extensions at ceiling level if possible. This will make the cords more evident, and helps to lessen the likelihood that someone might trip. That is why the cordless models have become so popular—the cord problem has been eliminated altogether. If the tools do have cords, be sure to use a grounded plug.

Handheld Power Tools
Maintenance Schedule

	Drill	Saber saw	Circular saw	Biscuit joiner
Serial #				
Date of Purchase:				
Maintenance Notes:				

A single maintenance schedule can be made for all of the handheld power tools. In this way nothing will be forgotten at the appointed maintenance time, usually from three to six months.

Safety Rules

- Let each tool come to full power before beginning the operation.
- Make sure that the work is supported or clamped down well.
- Make sure that all chucks, collets, blade clamps and fence clamps are tightened properly.
- Be sure that there is a wooden "buffer board" under the work when drilling through the piece.
- Drill a "starter hole" for all inside cuts to be made with the saber saw.
- Keep all saw and biscuit joiner bases flat on the work piece.
- Always remove loose jewelry or clothing that could be easily snagged or caught by the tool.
- Always pay attention to power and extension cords.
- Never put your hand in front of where you are cutting.
- Always tie long hair back or tuck it in your hat.
- Never operate any power tool without eye protection.

HANDHELD POWER TOOL LOCATION

These tools come ready to use, "No assembly required." The proper blade or bit need only be installed for the particular operation at hand. This will leave some time to meditate on an overview of convenient placement. The handheld power tools should all be located in one centralized place.

A drill motor will either be outfitted with an adjustable chuck or a collet. The smaller high-speed drills usually use the collet.

This is a matter of good shop organization for efficiency's sake. A carpeted shelf under the workbench makes a great place to store these tools. If that is not possible, try to find a cabinet or area where they all can be stored together.

HANDHELD POWER TOOL MAINTENANCE

Like the portable sanders, this is another area where the tools can be grouped together into one maintenance schedule program (page 133). A time period of three to six months, depending on the operation, can be assigned for the general maintenance of the group. In this way nothing will be forgotten or overlooked. The saws will obviously require a different approach than the drills, but all of the notes can be taken at the same time in case parts will have to be ordered, etc.

One real good rule of thumb would be to always blow out the motor vents with compressed air. Sawdust and other dirt are very abrasive and can cause premature wear on the motor windings. This should be done on a weekly basis to really be effective. You do not have to note this on the schedule, but it is a good habit to get into. As far as the rest of it goes, I like to clean and lubricate the moving parts after each four hours of use if that occurs before my scheduled maintenance date.

HANDHELD POWER TOOL ADJUSTMENT AND ALIGNMENT

Most all of the handheld power tools are fairly simple in terms of design and moving parts. There are a few "bells and whistles" renditions, which always come supplied with owner's manuals to explain any differences. For the most part, common sense when setting the tools down is the best way to maintain good alignment. Often made of plastics, the casements, or shells, of the tools are more prone to damage than the larger machines.

The drill motor is basically a direct-drive tool. Even the right-angle types are driven directly via a transmission. The spindle itself must be true and straight, and the chuck (or collet), which holds the bits, should expand and reduce with relative ease (top page 134). Most drills today have a variable-speed switch that needs to be kept clean—and sometimes replaced. With the saber saw, the blade must be responsive to the switch. The drive shaft, which has a blade screw and clamp at the end (top right), must be perfectly straight and well lubricated. The biscuit joiner is the most complicated of the bunch. The springs that return the base to the forward position (figure 10-8) must be replaced at times. The base itself should move smoothly during the cut. The fence/height gauge does have finite adjustments, and must move freely within the guides. The handheld circular saw also has more than one concern. The guard and spring must always be kept in perfect working order (top page 136). The saw base, which has adjustments for depth and angle of cut, must be well lubricated at the pivots, and the position locks must be well adjusted.

Each of the handheld power tools must be adjusted when installing the bit or blade, and sometimes there are base and fence adjustments. Read the manuals to learn how these adjustments are made.

The blade for the saber saw is held onto the shaft with a screw-and-clamp arrangement. The screw usually goes through a hole in the blade.

The biscuit joiner base is returned to position by the use of springs within the base. For most models, these springs are disconnected while installing the blade.

Adjustments

1. Drill motors
   - How the chuck or collet is tightened around the bit.
   - How the variable-speed feature is employed.
   - How the trigger is locked for continuous use.
   - How the reversing feature is employed.
2. Saber saws
   - How the blade is held onto the drive shaft.
   - How the base is adjusted for angle and locked.
   - How the trigger is locked for continuous use.
3. Handheld circular saws
   - How the blade is held on the arbor.
   - How the base is adjusted for angle.
   - How the base is adjusted for depth.
4. Biscuit joiners
   - How the blade mounts to the arbor.
   - How the fence is adjusted for height.
   - How the fence pivots for angle (optional feature).
   - How the base depth stop is employed.

DRILL MOTOR ALIGNMENT

The switch and drive spindle are the most important relationships of the drill motor. When a switch goes bad, it will either fail altogether or begin to short out slowly before failing. The drive spindle either has a collet or accepts a chuck that can be replaced if bent. If the actual spindle becomes bent,

It is very important that the guard of the portable circular saw is kept in good operating condition at all times. Among other things, this guard protects against injury from kickback.

Some drill motors have a switch that reverses the motor direction. These switches are not typically located; it is a matter of the manufacturer's placement.

chances are that it will be cheaper to replace the entire drill motor than to have the spindle replaced. One last concern with most drill motors would be the motor brushes, which should be turned periodically and replaced when they become too small.

Switches

With the exception of some variable-speed switches, a simple trigger switch can be replaced right in your shop. The part can be ordered directly from the manufacturer (most have 800 service numbers). If the switch is a complex variable type, it is wisest to have the tool repaired professionally, because there are a lot of insulation and polarization concerns. For those drills with reversing capabilities (bottom page 136), these are wired into the main trigger, and should also be sent out of shop for repair. The main thing to protect against is that the switch does not become misaligned or bent into the case. Be sure to blow the switch out frequently with compressed air, which helps to protect against early failure. It is also important to note that drill switches usually work in conjunction with a switch lock; once engaged, it should disengage when the trigger is depressed.

Drive Shafts

As mentioned, the spindle itself is the most critical part of the drill motor. It is often an extension of the motor shaft. If bent, the entire motor windings and shaft will have to be replaced. The alignment of the shaft can be checked by placing the drill motor in a padded vise with the chuck in a level position.

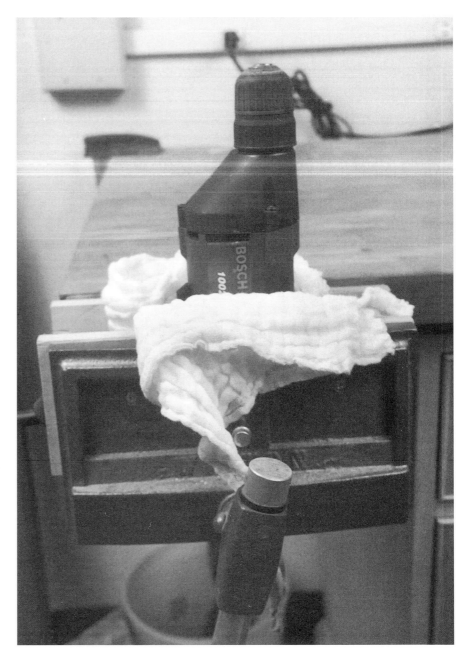

The drill motor can be placed in a padded vise to check for runout. The drill must first be leveled if a dial indicator is to be used.

The chuck or collet nut should be removed once the drill has been confirmed to be level (above). Use a dial indicator to check for runout while turning the shaft by hand.

SABER SAW ALIGNMENT

The saber saw has two basic functions that will need attention. The blade must move up and down smoothly and without a lot of play.

The base, which rests on the wood, should pivot smoothly so that the saw blade can be set to a desired angle to the material being cut. There are also some newer models that have the added feature of adjustable blade positioning. All of these concerns, along with motor brushes, should be noted on the maintenance schedule and checked at the appointed time.

Adjusting the Saber Saw Base

The adjustable saw base will pivot a total of 90° (top right). There will be an angle indicator at one end of the base that shows 45° in each direction. This scale can be set by first squaring the blade to the base and setting the scale indicator to 0°. Once set, all other indications should be correct. The base will have some means by which it can be locked at the desired position. Any movement here will yield a cut that is not square or of consistent angle. The base pivot area should be kept well oiled, being careful not to get any in the area of the base locking nut.

CIRCULAR SAW ALIGNMENT

As mentioned, the handheld circular saw can be considered a portable version of the table saw. There are no built-in fences or miter slides, but the saw base is often used in conjunction with a fence that is clamped to the work itself. Adjustment-wise, the base of the saw has two adjustments and two adjustment locks which are important. The depth of cut adjustment will determine how deep the blade penetrates into or below the material being cut (bottom right). The angle of cut adjustment will determine the angle at which the blade is set to the base (top page 139). The locks for both of these adjustment concerns must be in good working order. The worm gear models, and some of the more expensive direct-drive models, do have a tension adjustment associated with the locks. This is just a matter of tightening a nut on the lock itself for added lock sensitiv-

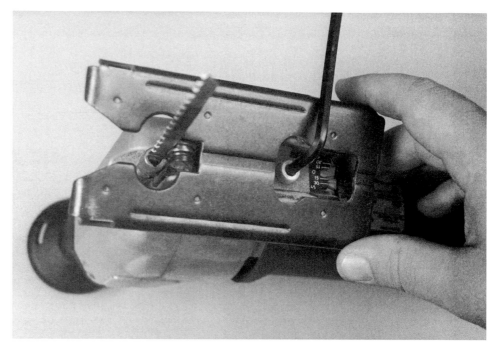

The saber saw base is adjustable for angle of cut. Each manufacturer's model will have a slightly different means of adjustment. Be sure that the base has been clamped after angle adjustment is made.

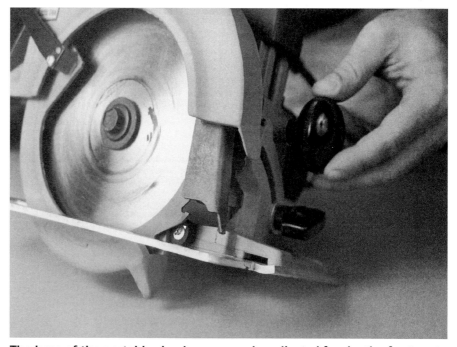

The base of the portable circular saw can be adjusted for depth of cut up to approximately one-half the diameter of the blade. It is very important that the depth lock be secured after each adjustment.

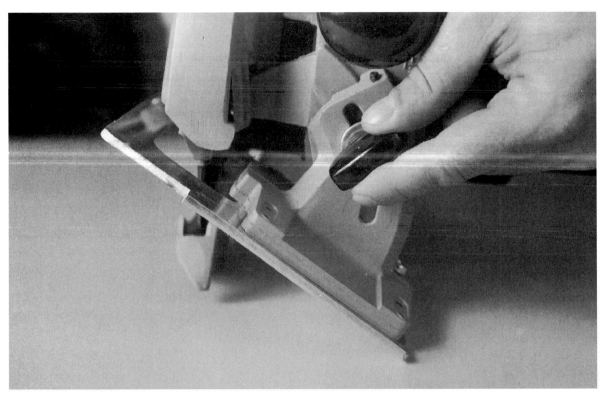

The base of the portable circular saw can also be adjusted for angle of cut. This is adjustable in one direction only; so the saw must be positioned accordingly on the work.

ity, and will be explained in the owner's manual.

The motor brushes should be rotated every three to four hours of use, and changed when they become less than ⅜″ long. This is important to both the longevity of the brushes and the motor itself. The motor bearings are sealed and need no additional oiling. Use the best grade of nondetergent oil (SAE 20) to lubricate the shaft where it meets the tool body.

BISCUIT JOINER ALIGNMENT

In terms of moving parts, the biscuit joiner is the most complicated of the handheld power tools. The circular saw blade is mounted to an arbor and is sandwiched between the movable base. With most biscuit joiners, the base

springs must be disconnected or removed to install the blade. The base/fence combination adjusts up or down for height of cut, and sometimes has a pivoting feature for angle of cut. The depth of cut is governed by a dial or cam type of adjustment that can be preset for each of the three biscuit sizes. There are spring-loaded pins in the leading edge of the base that keep the tool from slipping during the cutting process. These pins should be kept lightly oiled and moving freely. If they do not retract within the base, the blade will not cut to full depth.

The Blade and Arbor

As mentioned, the blade is mounted to an arbor within the base. If the blade is warped or the arbor has a great deal of runout,

the slot will be cut wider than the biscuit can expand. This is a critical tolerance, and the most important function of the tool. Any discrepancy here will be noticed when the biscuit appears to be sloppy within the slot before the glue has been applied. If this problem becomes evident, the source must be traced. First, check that the blade is not dull or warped. A dull blade will sometimes overheat and warp while cutting. If the blade proves to be in good shape, runout will have to be checked on the flange of the arbor. If runout is any more than .005″ on the flange, the tool should be repaired professionally. Be sure that the arbor flange is clean before a dial indicator reading is taken.

The most important adjustment on a biscuit joiner is the height of cut. This is adjusted by moving the base/fence parallel to the blade per the thickness of the material being slotted.

The Movable Base

The base retracts and returns with the help of the base springs (above). These springs will most likely have to be disconnected when sliding the base back for blade installation. The guides on the sliding base must be cleaned and oiled frequently to keep the tool moving smoothly. Blow the base out with compressed air between oiling to prevent sawdust from building up.

The Adjustable Base Fence

The fence part of the base must adjust for height smoothly and evenly. If the fence is not adjusted exactly parallel to the blade, the part halves will not reference correctly when the biscuit is installed. There is usually a numbered scale on each side of the fence that will make this an easy adjustment. A more important concern is that the fence clamps are tight once the height has been set. Tighten the screws to these clamps periodically so that they do not become ineffective. One final thing regarding the base: There will be some kind of center indicator mark which is the reference point for all cuts. This should be kept visible by a touch of red paint or, better yet, red fingernail polish.

The Handheld Power Tools
Troubleshooting at a Glance

1. The portable drill motor

PROBLEM	SOLUTION
Drilled hole is not round, or is frayed at the top of the cut	Increase the speed of the drill and check that the bit is not dull
Drill motor does not function	Rotate the motor brushes and check the cord for breaks in the line

2. The saber saw

PROBLEM	SOLUTION
Cut is not square or of consistent angle	Be sure that the blade is not dull or bent, and check that the saw base is locked into position
Saw does not function	Rotate the motor brushes and check the cord for breaks in the line

3. The circular saw

PROBLEM	SOLUTION
Blade does not cut at a constant angle or depth	Check that lockdown clamps are secured at desired angle and depth
Saw does not function	Rotate the motor brushes and check the cord for breaks in the line

4. The biscuit joiner

PROBLEM	SOLUTION
Part halves do not register	Check that adjustable fence height is parallel with the blade
Cut is not the proper depth	Check that the spring-loaded base pins are retracting all of the way into the base
Cut is too wide for the biscuits	Check that the blade is not dull or warped, and that there is not excessive runout on the arbor flange

HANDHELD POWER TOOL
ALL TOOLS:

✔ Correct bit or blade is installed and tightened
✔ Tool is plugged into a grounded circuit
✔ There are no cords or obstructions in the way
✔ Safety glasses and face mask are on

DRILL MOTORS:

✔ Motor is switched to correct direction
✔ Drill bit is marked for depth of cut
✔ Motor is set to correct speed

SABER SAW:

✔ Base angle is set and locked
✔ Saw is set at correct speed

CIRCULAR SAW:

✔ Saw base is set and locked to proper depth
✔ Saw base is set and locked to proper angle

BISCUIT JOINER:

✔ Fence is set to proper height
✔ Base is set for proper depth of cut
✔ Material is marked for joiner register

Index